Economic Diversification in Africa

A REVIEW OF SELECTED COUNTRIES

OECD

This work is published on the responsibility of the Secretary-General of the OECD. The opinions expressed and arguments employed herein do not necessarily reflect the official views of the Organisation or of the governments of its member countries.

Please cite this publication as:

OECD/United Nations (2011), *Economic Diversification in Africa: A Review of Selected Countries*, OECD Publishing.

http://dx.doi.org/10.1787/9789264038059-en

ISBN 978-92-64-03805-9 (print)
ISBN 978-92-64-09623-3 (PDF)

Corrigenda to OECD publications may be found on line at: *www.oecd.org/publishing/corrigenda*.

Foreword

Ihe global financial and economic crisis has revealed Africa's vulnerability to external economic shocks. Largely dependent on the export of commodities, many of the continent's economies suffered setbacks in economic growth and in their efforts to meet the Millennium Development Goals by 2015.

Economic diversification holds great potential to increase Africa's resilience and would contribute to achieving and sustaining long term economic growth and development in the continent. Broadly-based economies, active in a wide range of sectors, and firmly integrated into their regions, are better able to generate robust growth and sustainable growth.

However, the expansion of activities in underdeveloped sectors, or indeed the development of new activities, is a significant challenge and requires a combined effort by African governments, the private sector and the international community. In addition, and in light of the small size of many African economies, a regional approach to economic diversification is imperative to reap the benefits of larger domestic markets and economies of scale.

This study analyses the economies of selected African countries' and their diversification profiles and strategies. The five case studies, of Angola, Benin, Kenya, South Africa, and Tunisia, provide a detailed view on the state of economic diversification in the continent. From these experiences, policy recommendations are drawn for African governments, regional institutions and the international community.

Economic diversification in Africa can deliver the improved utilization of the continent's vast agricultural and mineral resources. Minerals processing, the expansion of manufacturing activities, the production and export of non-traditional agricultural and industrial products, and the further development of services sectors such as tourism, will all improve Africa's economic prospects.

Setting African economies on a more balanced, broad-based and diversified growth path will not be easy. A conducive business environment, responsible management of natural resources and good governance are all indispensable to support private enterprises, harness their innovative potential, and implement other innovative ideas put forward in this study.

Cheick Sidi Diarra	Angel Gurria	Ibrahim Mayaki
United Nations	Secretary-General	Chief Executive Officer
Under-Secretary-General	Organisation for Economic	NEPAD Planning
and Special Adviser	Co-operation	and Co-ordinating
on Africa	and Development (OECD)	Agency

Acknowledgements

The original draft of this study was prepared by John HE Maré, a South Africa-based consultant. Subsequent updates have been undertaken and comments and suggestions have been provided by Kerri Elgar, Said Kechida, Dambudzo Muzenda and Mike Pfister (NEPAD-OECD Africa Investment Initiative), and Olivier Schwank , Katrin Toomel and Juliet Wasswa-Mugambwa (UN Office of the Special Adviser on Africa). The study also benefited from comments by Ben Idrissa Ouedraogo and David Wright, (UN Office of the Special Adviser on Africa). Carol Sakubita (UN OSAA) provided logistic support. The work was carried out under the overall direction and guidance of David Mehdi Hamam, Chief, Policy Analysis and Monitoring Unit, UN OSAA and Karim Dahou, Executive Manager, NEPAD-OECD Africa Investment Initiative.

The report was enriched by the discussions at the Expert Group Meeting on Economic Diversification in Africa: A Review of Selected Countries, held in Addis Ababa, in November 2009, with the participation of: Abdalla Hamdok, Emmanuel Nnadozie, Joseph Atta-Mensah (United Nations Economic Commission for Africa); Festus Fajana, Merah Nadir, Inye Nathan Briggs (African Union Commission); Ibrahim Gourouza (New Partnership for Africa's Development Agency); Richard Randriamandrato, Jamel Boujdaria, Dotun Ajayi, (Regional Economic Communities); El Iza Mohamedou (African Development Bank); Karim Dahou (Organisation for Economic Co-operation and Development); Fidele Sarassoro (United Nations Development Programme); Aurelia Calabro (United Nations Industrial Development Organisation); Youssef Chaitani (United Nations Economic and Social Commission for Western Africa); Mumbi Kiereini (Kenya Private Sector Alliance); and Alemayehu Geda (Addis Ababa University).

Table of Contents

Figures

List of Acronyms

ABR	Africa Business Roundtable
ACP	African, Caribbean and Pacific
AfDB	African Development Bank
AGOA	Africa Growth and Opportunity Act
APRM	African Peer Review Mechanism (of the NEPAD process)
ASEAN	Association of South East Asian Nations
ASGISA	Accelerated and Shared Growth Initiative for South Africa
AU	African Union
BDA	Banco de Desenvolvimento de Angola-BDA (Angolan Development Bank)
BUSA	Business Unity South Africa
CAADP	The Comprehensive Africa Agriculture Development Programme
CAD	The China Africa Development Bank
CBI	Cross Border Initiative
CEN-SAD	Community of Sahel-Saharan States
CHAMSA	Chambers of Commerce and Industry South Africa
COMESA	Common Market for Eastern and Southern Africa
DBSA	Development Bank of Southern Africa
DRC	Democratic Republic of Congo
DTI	Department of Trade and Industry (of South Africa)
EAC	East African Community
EASSy	Eastern Africa Submarine Cable System
EBA	Everything But Arms
ECCAS	Economic Community of Central African States
ECGLC	Economic Community of the Great Lakes Countries
ECOWAS	Economic Community of West African States
EPA	Economic Partnership Agreement
ERS	Economic Recovery Strategy
ESIPP	EU SADC Investment Promotion Programme
EU	European Union
FES	Friedrich Ebert Stiftung
FND	Fundo Nasional de Desenvolvimento (National Development Fund)

FTA	Free Trade Agreement
GDP	Gross Domestic Product
GEAR	Growth, Employment and Redistribution Strategy
HCDA	Horticultural Crop Development Agency
ICT	Information and Communications Technology
IDC	Industrial Development Corporation
IGD	Institute for Global Dialogue
IGAD	Intergovernmental Authority on Development
ILO	International Labour Organisation
IPAP	Industrial Policy Action Plan
LDC	Least Developed Country
MEDA	Mediterranean Economic Development Agreement
MERCOSUR	Common Market of the South
MIDP	Motor Industry Development Program
MFN	Most Favoured Nation
NBF	NEPAD Business Foundation
NBG	NEPAD Business Group
NEDLAC	National Economic Development and Labour Council
NEPAD	New Partnership for Africa's Development
NESC	National Economic and Social Council
NIPF	National Industrial Policy Framework
NGO	Non Governmental Organisation
PPP	Public-Private Partnerships/Projects
RDP	Reconstruction and Development Programme
REC(s)	Regional Economic Community/ies
RIDS	Regional Industrial Development Strategy
SABS	South African Bureau of Standards
ACOB	South African Chamber of Business
SACU	Southern African Customs Union
SADC	Southern African Development Community
SADCBF	Southern African Development Community (SADC) Business Forum
SDI	Spatial Development Initiative
SDP	Spatial Development Programme
SME	Small Medium Scale Enterprise
SSA	Sub-Saharan Africa
SWA	Sovereign Wealth Fund
TDCA	Trade, Co-operation and Development Agreement
TICAD	Tokyo International Conference for African Development
UN	United Nations
UNECA	United Nations Economic Commission for Africa
UNIDO	United Nations Industrial Development Organisation

UNOSAA	United Nations Office of the Adviser on Africa
USD	United States Dollar
WTO	World Trade Organisation
ZAR	South African Rand

Executive Summary

The global financial and economic crises exposed one of the major weaknesses of a number of African economies: their dependence on too few export commodities and one or two sectors. Such dependence makes many countries vulnerable to fluctuations in commodity prices, demand and extreme weather events such as droughts and floods. This study looks at how African governments can diversify their economies and analyses five countries' economic diversification profiles in particular. It begins by examining some of the major determinants of diversification and also looks at how the private sector plays a key role by being at the forefront of innovation, research and development and production. Good governance is needed to create an enabling environment for investment and trade; to manage natural resources; and to set policies to develop strategic sectors. A regional approach to economic diversification is particularly important, especially given the small size of African economies and the benefits of economies of scale from regional initiatives. New economic partnerships, including South-South co-operation and relations, offer Africa the opportunity to expand its economic options. Lastly, infrastructure and human resources help to facilitate trade, productivity and innovation and are key drivers of diversification.

Diversifying African economies is not an easy task. One of the key challenges is how to overcome over-specialisation, whereby some countries have developed systems and know-how for one specific area of the economy but find it difficult to transfer these to other sectors and activities. Also, significant trade barriers exist and African firms may not be able to compete against their peers in other parts of the world because of lack of access to finance, administrative hurdles, weak productive capacities, and other impediments to competitiveness. These challenges need to be addressed if diversification efforts are to gain traction.

This study looks at the economies of five African countries to analyse their diversification profiles and strategies. It starts with relatively well-diversified South Africa which nonetheless faces constraints in its human resources and labour markets; followed by Kenya, which has made great strides in boosting certain sectors such as tourism and telecommunications. It continues with Tunisia's example of successful diversification efforts and Angola, which depends on oil revenues to fuel growth. The final case study deals with Benin, a country which is dependent on cotton but has a favourable policy environment and a record of good governance that could lead to private sector development and investments in other sectors.

Chapter 1

Introduction to Economic Diversification

1.1. Overview

For more than a decade, African countries have been enjoying high levels of economic growth, human development, and political stability. As they continue along the path of economic progress, it is imperative that they find ways to diversify their economies, namely by strengthening non-traditional sectors; expanding their range of products and exports; and engaging with new economic and development partners.

Diversification does not occur in a vacuum. There needs to be an enabling environment to make diversification possible. A number of key drivers have already been identified, for example by the 2007 UNECA Economic Report on Africa, including investment, trade and industrial policies; a dynamic growth performance; macroeconomic stability, a competitive exchange rate and expansionary but responsible fiscal policy; and institutional variables such as good governance and absence of conflict.[1] This study will focus mainly on the investment, governance and regional dimensions of economic diversification as well as on human and natural resources. The role of infrastructure, with emphasis on transport and energy,[2] will also be taken into account.

In addition, the private sector has an important role to play in its own right and in conjunction with the Government. Similarly, regional economic institutions such as Regional Economic Communities (RECs) and other international partners help contribute to Africa's economic priorities, including through reinforcing the public sector's capacities to implement policies and reforms conducive to diversification.

Of course, many challenges arise when pursuing a diversification strategy. It is often necessary to make significant investments in human resources and infrastructure to support economic sectors and activities such as value-addition in commodities. These are long-term endeavours that need government commitment and political will, not to mention major capital investments. Moreover, in pursuing new sectors, products and partners, African governments must be careful not to neglect their traditional economic bases.

There are many benefits that could arise from more diversified economies: less exposure to external shocks; an increase in trade; higher productivity of capital and labour; and better regional economic integration.[3] These benefits, in addition to effective public management, can help to reduce poverty and promote human and social development.

Diversification nevertheless remains limited in most African countries, with only a few success stories. Chapter 2 of this report will focus on the five selected case studies of Angola, Benin, Kenya, South Africa, and Tunisia to illustrate how these African countries have implemented economic diversification strategies. The chapter will highlight key actions and policies that have been pursued by these national governments in the quest for economic diversification, as well as the challenges and successes encountered. It will also analyse the linkages made with regional economies in efforts to boost trade. These five cases represent a range of country profiles, from resource-rich Angola, to relatively well-diversified South Africa and Tunisia, promising Kenya and resource-poor Benin. In each example, governance and public policies have played a strong role in accelerating diversification.

Chapter 3 of this study provides conclusions and recommendations, with particular emphasis on the role of government and other decision-making entities and relevant stakeholders.

1.2. Major Determinants

A. Governance

Good governance is a pre-requisite in building an enabling environment for economic diversification. This involves designing and implementing policies to nurture fledgling sectors and ensuring that they can be developed in an environment that allows them to flourish and contribute more to the national economy. At the regional level, there needs to be efficient co-ordination among different decision-makers and stakeholders in the regional and global economic environment. These national and regional, public and private, individual and institutional leaders constitute the "executive drivers" that shape the governance framework for diversification.

Executive drivers are important for diversification in many ways. One is through the prudent economic management of natural resources. Also, the Government has an important role to play in establishing the regulatory framework that supports economic activity to ensure a healthy business climate. This is particularly important because many African countries, unlike their counterparts in the developed world, often have weak private sectors and industries, making them more dependent on government interventions to thrive. Of course, the public service needs increased institutional capacity to implement business-friendly reforms.

One example of such government action is the reform of customs procedures and loosening administrative burdens for trade so that it is easier for manufacturers to export their products and import goods. As Table 1.1 shows, Africa is not as competitive as comparable regions on a host of trading regulations. The high cost of importing and exporting, along with lengthy time

Table 1.1. **Trading regulations in SSA and case study countries**

Region/Economy	Documents to export (#)	Time to export (days)	Cost to export (USD per container)	Documents to import (#)	Time to import (days)	Cost to import (USD per container)
Sub-Saharan Africa	7.8	33.6	1 941.8	8.8	39.4	2 365.4
Eastern Europe and Central Asia	6.5	26.8	1 581.8	7.8	28.4	1 773.5
Latin America and Caribbean	6.8	18.6	1 243.6	7.3	20.9	1 481.0
Middle East and North Africa	6.4	22.5	1 034.8	7.4	25.9	1 221.7
South Asia	8.5	32.4	1 364.1	9.0	32.2	1 509.1
Angola	11.0	65.0	2 250.0	8.0	59.0	3 240.0
Benin	7.0	30.0	1 251.0	7.0	32.0	1 400.0
Kenya	9.0	27.0	2 055.0	8.0	25.0	2 190.0
South Africa	8.0	30.0	1 531.0	9.0	35.0	1 807.0
Tunisia	5.0	15.0	783.0	7.0	21.0	858.0

Source: Adapted from the World Bank's "Doing Business" 2010 report.

delays and cumbersome administrative process, make it difficult for African enterprises to increase trade volumes and discourages them from expanding their product base in the first place. At a regional level, national economies need to harmonise their standards to ensure that goods and labour can move freely across borders.

Government intervention is also important when responding to economic developments that offer opportunities for increasing diversification. For example, the global financial crisis has led to a drop in the prices of commodities, and has affected African countries which rely solely or predominantly on a few, or even one commodity. This was the case for Botswana, for example, where diamond sales dropped sharply. But the Government of Botswana, which is widely considered to be one of the best-run economies in Africa, was able to mount a swift response, with the help of a USD 1.5 billion loan from the African Development Bank (AfDB). Part of this response included a strategy for diversifying the economy away from diamonds by creating a number of "hubs", or economic areas, as part of this strategy (Box 1.1). This is an example of how government action can drive diversification.

B. Role of the private sector

The private sector can also play a role in advancing diversification, by driving innovation and economic activity in under-exploited sectors. It can, for example, invest in Research and Development for new activities. Moreover, private companies often stand at the frontier of new sectors and bring innovation to the economy. But many enterprises in Africa are informal, small-scale, and lack access to capital, making it difficult for them to fully exploit business

> ## Box 1.1. **Six hubs to spearhead diversification in Botswana**
>
> During NDP 9, and currently in NDP 10, the Government has identified areas to focus on for enhanced economic growth and diversification. The following six "hubs" were created:
>
> The Education Hub seeks to increase the quality and relevance of education at all levels and, thereby, make Botswana more competitive by attracting leading tertiary institutions, scholars, researchers and students into the country.
>
> The Innovation Hub is aimed at creating a platform for local and foreign businesses engaged in R&D and knowledge intensive activities (i.e. ICT). It will also establish an incubator for start-up companies and facilitate networking amongst businesses.
>
> The Agricultural Hub will encourage participation in farming, mentor farmers on agribusiness skills, and endeavour to commercialise the agricultural sector in an effort to make the industry more sustainable.
>
> The Diamond Hub intends to establish a diamond trade centre for rough/polished diamonds and to promote sustainable downstream activities such as polishing and jewellery making.
>
> The Medical Hub hopes to identify projects and programmes that will make Botswana a centre of excellence in the provision of healthcare services. It will also outsource certain hospitals in an effort to attract specialists and optimise the quality of the health facilities.
>
> The Transport Hub seeks to re-position the country as a regional hub for rail, road and air transport, and to support a competitive transport and logistics industry in Botswana.
>
> Note: According to the AfDB project report, the National Development Plans (NDPs) are "the main instruments for implementing the policies and programmes to achieve Vision 2016, the country's long term perspective plan. NDP 10 covers the period April 2009-March 2016 and seeks to translate the Vision 2016 objectives into concrete policies and actions... The strategic thrust of NDP 10 is to accelerate diversification of the economy, as a means of reducing poverty and expanding employment creation."
>
> Source: Economic Diversification Support Loan: Botswana Appraisal Report, AfDB, 8 May 2009.

opportunities. In this case, the Government should find ways to strengthen entrepreneurship, by creating favourable industrial and trade policies and eliminating bureaucratic obstacles to starting businesses. Governments should be sensitive to the needs of the private sector, such as by improving the business climate through "outreach" for constructive partnerships with the private sector.

Similarly, the private sector should reciprocate by engaging with government initiatives and should take the lead in driving the agenda for diversifying the economy.[4] There is no shortage of business opportunities in Africa (Box 1.2) and the private sector is best placed to exploit them.

> ## Box 1.2. **Africa's business opportunities**
>
> In the last three to four years, Africa has seen the increase of new investment in non-resource-based sectors such as tourism, manufacturing, financial services, telecommunications and construction. In fact, the largest opportunity lies in consumer-related sectors, which are growing two to three times faster than those in developed countries. This group alone – which comprises consumer goods, banking, and telecommunications among others – could generate as much as USD 1.4 trillion in consumer spending by 2020 – compared to Africa's combined GDP of USD 1.8 trillion in 2008 and projected USD 2.6 trillion in 2020. The growth in consumer-related sectors will be driven by the rising rates of urbanisation, with 40% of Africans living in urban cities, which is higher than in India and close to China's levels. Also, the number of households with disposable income is expected to rise by 50% in the next 10 years. These factors offer the opportunity for African economies to become more varied, as they adjust to the needs of the consumer class. Moreover, the rate of return on investment is higher in Africa than in any other developing region and governments have implemented macroeconomic policies to create a stable and conducive environment for doing business. All the same, some significant risks remain and African countries need to put in place more reforms to facilitate economic activities. But certainly, Africa's bright outlook for business bodes well for the diversification of its economies.
>
> Source: *Lions on the Move: The Progress and Potential of African Economies*, McKinsey Global Institute, June 2010.

C. *Natural resources*

Among the various factors that have the potential to drive economic diversification, a country's natural resources are crucially important. These resources can be exploited to increase the range of exports and goods a country produces, especially through beneficiation, whereby additional value can be created from the resources extracted. However, Africa's great potential is often unrealised because of suboptimal government management of natural resources and a failure to use the gains from resource exploitation to further other economic activities. For example, the profits from exporting minerals can be used to develop manufacturing, tourism and services, thereby broadening the country's economic base.

Natural resources have been the key sector for economic growth in Africa: the continent has been traditionally driven by exports of agricultural goods and primary products such as minerals and hydro-carbons. However, countries dependent on just a few commodities for their revenue are vulnerable to boom and bust cycles as the prices of commodities are subject to wide fluctuations. Therefore, the need for expanding the beneficiation of such products, and seeking sustainable utilisation where possible, are priorities for African economic growth and diversification.[5] If accompanied by policies that encourage trade and exports, the exploitation of natural resources could provide improved opportunities for African countries to produce and trade a variety of goods within Africa, and in the global market.

Subsequent trade and investment flows would therefore feed the momentum for further economic diversification[6] as traded goods would increasingly be composed of non-traditional agricultural and industrial products.

D. Regional factors

Regional integration is an important strategy for facilitating trade and commerce. This includes reforming customs administration systems to make it easier for entrepreneurs to transport their goods freely. It also consists in Spatial Development Initiatives (SDIs) or Spatial Development Programmes (SDPs), which are usually trans-frontier in format and have transport corridors as their main component. They are largely driven by RECs and national governments with strong support from key African development institutions such as the African Development Bank (AfDB) and the Development Bank of Southern Africa (DBSA). By their nature, spatial initiatives aim to promote growth by increasing the diversity of the various national economies in which the SDPs are located and stimulate cross-border economic activity and regional economic integration.

Because many African countries share certain geographic features such as river basins, mountain ranges and lakes, and because of the small size of the domestic market, regional integration becomes an important aspect of any economic growth and diversification strategy. Some countries have overlapping memberships in regional associations.

Tanzania, for instance, is a member of both the East African Community (EAC) and the Southern African Development Community. Similarly, Angola is linked to regional organisations from both Central and Southern Africa. However, cross-cutting regional and geographic associations need not be a liability for these and other countries. A number of North African countries have taken advantage of both their geographic location in North Africa and their proximity to the European and Mediterranean markets. Tunisia, for example, has strong economic ties to the Mediterranean region and the EU, and Algeria has strong ties to both the Mediterranean region and to Saudi Arabia and Jordan in the Middle East. These countries have increased their access to multiple regional economic spheres which can serve as markets for their products. This, in turn, could potentially broaden domestic production and fuel diversification.

Strengthening regional integration among African economies includes harmonising various technological standards and regulations, and reforming customs and border controls. These measures are critical for strengthening the business climate in Africa. Regional integration is especially important given the small size of most African states and their economies.

Since the early seventies, regional institutions have been identified as key "executive drivers"[7] of development. RECs hold a significant position in terms of promoting regional economic integration in Africa as they form the pillars of the continent's integration since the establishment of the African Economic Community (AEC).

RECs can lay the foundations for economic diversification by creating common markets, pooling resources, and providing a framework to coordinate the regional management of infrastructure such as transportation corridors, energy and natural resources. They can also help to strengthen capacities related to regional human resources, health, security and the environment.

Unfortunately, there are many challenges that undermine RECs' potential as catalysts for regional integration and economic diversification, including overlapping memberships among member countries; the lack of political will; the lack of compensation mechanisms; the fear over loss of sovereignty; and weak infrastructure and financial environments. Much can be gained by synchronising national initiatives relevant to diversification with the governance structures and priorities of RECs, as is well illustrated by the alignment of many national plans with the SDIs/SDPs of the AfDB. Certainly, there are numerous benefits from regional co-operation and integration given the many shared interests among African countries, ranging from trans-border disease control to immigration, security, and transport systems.

E. The broader international framework

The international context is of increasing relevance for all African economies and offers the prospect of an operative environment that can spur national economic diversification. Economies like China, India, Japan, the European Union (EU) and USA can act as key partners for African countries in economic diversification. Such partnerships could take a number of forms including joint business ventures, investment and trade agreements, technology transfers and capacity building for an improved business climate.

Their role in creating expanded markets for African products is particularly important for improved diversification in Africa, but this is complicated by market access issues and African capacity to take advantage of international business opportunities.

There are other facets of international co-operation that can have an impact on economic diversification. Various international assistance programmes aimed at Africa's economic development, for example, have increasingly emphasised strengthening business activities. However, there is potential to significantly increase support for economic diversification and boost capacities to best exploit market opportunities. In this respect, international programmes have the potential to help build the kind of domestic leadership inside African countries that can help improve economic diversification.

Among the primary vehicles for broadening the scope of national economies are trade agreements. For instance, the EU has been providing trade preferences to the African, Caribbean and Pacific Countries under the Yaoundé and the Lomé Conventions since 1963. These relations are being adapted to the multilateral trading rules of the WTO through the negotiations of the Economic Partnership Agreements (EPAs) with four African regional groupings. In addition, the Everything but Arms (EBA) Initiative, which allows duty-free access for all exports from Least Developed Countries (LDCs), except arms, is a key factor supporting diversification in these economies. The October 2007 launch of the EU-Africa Partnership on Infrastructure is especially noteworthy and includes a prioritisation of African continental infrastructure projects. It aims to facilitate regional economic integration and diversification, and includes areas such as energy, science, the information society and space.

The USA's African Growth and Opportunity Act (AGOA) (see Box 1.3) is another important agreement that has had a great effect on stimulating diversification in African economies by opening expanded markets in the USA to African exports.

Box 1.3. **African Growth and Opportunity Act (AGOA)**

The African Growth and Opportunity Act (AGOA) is a US government initiative to boost trade from African countries to the United States and encourage American businesses to explore trade opportunities in Africa. It provides for the removal of import duties and quotas as a way to allow countries to start exporting a wider range of products to the US. The initiative covers 6 000 product items, with 90% of products coming from three categories: energy-related, textiles and apparel, and transportation equipment. To be eligible for the AGOA, countries have to pass certain criteria, based on good governance and rule of law. Currently, 41 SSA countries are eligible, although those that backtrack on rule of law can have their benefits – such as Most Favored Nation status – terminated. AGOA has much potential to boost Africa's capacity to trade and to diversify and increase its exports. Indeed, two-way trade between the US and Africa has more than doubled since the legislation came into effect in 2000.

Source: AGOA.net, US State Department, 2010.

The EU and its member states remain the leading development and economic partners for Sub-Saharan Africa (SSA) in terms of funding. Therefore, economic diversification initiatives in SSA flowing from the EPAs could be backed by European assistance. Nevertheless, increased diplomatic efforts are needed on both sides for these ventures and to address ongoing challenges in furthering co-operation on economic diversification, including African governments' perceptions of the dangers that the EPAs' market access rules overly restrict African freedom of economic policy space, regional integration and development.

China is an important economic partner for Africa, as evidenced by the increase in trade, investment flows, and various forms of economic co-operation between the two sides in the past couple of decades. Whereas EU member countries were traditionally the major investors in Africa, along with the USA and to a lesser extent Japan, China has grown to become a major investor in African resource sectors and has facilitated the development of African infrastructure. Such infrastructure – roads, ports and power stations – can be used to support national and regional economic diversification and to boost supply chains. China's financial commitments to African infrastructure are also impressive: within four years, it had more than quadrupled from less than USD 1 billion per year in 2001-03 to USD 4.5 billion in 2007. At their peak, commitments reached USD 7 billion in 2006 (WB, 2008).[8]

The upsurge in Chinese funding for African infrastructure offers great opportunities for boosting Africa's growth. However, there have not been convincing plans thus far by African governments to ensure the economic relationship with China benefits a wide range of sectors at the national and regional levels.

Moreover, there needs to be greater capacity in the public sector to build on the investments made by Chinese companies, such as maintaining roads built by the Chinese or using Chinese finance (mostly concessional loans) to catalyse other resources and activities for development.

China is not the only active South-South economic partner in Africa. India has been playing an increasingly prominent role on the economic scene and Gulf countries have been similarly growing in importance. These actors and others have tremendous potential for Africa's economic development. As with the relatively new growth in Chinese economic ties with Africa, they represent new international partners that Africa can use to improve mechanisms to convert gains from the resources "boom" (and indeed, other economic outputs) for investing in long-term sustainable diversified economic activities both nationally and regionally.

F. Institutional capacity and human resources

In addition to other input factors, human resources and institutional capacity merit special consideration. Human and institutional capacities act as enablers – to facilitate supply chains, for example, and help unlock potential for diversification from resource-based and other sectors.

At a regional level institutional capacity and co-ordination is key for establishing regulatory frameworks for trans-national infrastructure, customs and coordinating overlapping memberships.

Human resources are important for boosting innovation in any economy, for example through R&D and management skills that lead to better products and economic processes. Again, the support of government and civil society can unlock the potential of human resources to contribute positively to economic diversification. This includes boosting tertiary education and supporting research and development in high-growth sectors. For example, the Japanese International Co-operation Agency (JICA) supported the development of Africa's first mobile phone factory in Zambia, in co-operation with a local Zambian company, Mobile Telecommunications, which led to a new phone brand called MTech. As part of the project, the company has trained local Zambians on technical assembling of mobile phones. They also plan to establish a design house and R&D centre on mobile phone technology, and to export their phones to the rest of the SADC and COMESA region.[9] The MTech initiative shows how partnerships with international agencies can lead to the development of new technologies and increase in the relevant skills on the part of locals.

1.3. Major challenges

A. Specialisation

Several academic studies have analysed the relationship between a country's economic growth and its levels of specialisation, from where a country produces a range of goods in few, concentrated sectors, to where this range broadens. There is evidence that at the early stages of economic development, where most African countries currently are, countries tend to leverage their natural endowments to boost economic gains from niche sectors. But as they prioritise new sectors, increase productivity and diversify their economies, they eventually reach relatively high levels of per-capita income. At this point of high development, countries then begin to specialise again.[10] These findings add weight to the case for diversification, and serve as a caution against the hasty pursuit of specialisation when economic growth levels are not sufficiently high.

B. International opportunities

At present, Africa accounts for about 3% of the world's GDP and world trade,[11] with a share in global manufactured exports close to zero. This weak integration in the global economy is a result of the failure of most countries in Africa to become competitive trading partners in a broader range of economic activities worldwide. However, African countries can embrace emerging opportunities such as by building economic partnerships with emerging markets through South-South co-operation. In addition, the Copenhagen climate change meetings in December 2009 have led to new possibilities of international support for "greening" African economic growth but existing mechanisms such as the Clean Development Mechanism, which provides emission reduction credits to private companies investing in sustainable energy projects in developing countries, is seldom used so far in Sub-Saharan Africa due to difficulties for the private sector to apply it in the current context over the continent. But institutional measures – such as establishing feed-in tariffs to make investment in renewable energy projects lucrative – could help to overcome private investors' reluctance to seize these new economic opportunities.

C. Trade barriers

Intra-African trade is quite low, and its external trade volumes and destinations not well-diversified. Some of the factors behind this include: "the economic structure of African countries, which constrains the supply of diversified products; poor institutional policies; weak infrastructure; weak financial and capital markets; and failure to put trade protocols in place".[12] External barriers to trade include the faltering progress in concluding the Doha Round, mainly because of lack of agreement over market access for agricultural goods, and the lack of progress in the negotiations over Economic Partnership Agreements (EPAs). Moreover, there are 15 landlocked countries in Africa and their distance from the sea raises their transportation costs and undercuts their export competitiveness. To address these problems, various African countries have made efforts to create common markets and there has been some success, including the launch of the COMESA customs unions and the Common Market of the East African Community (EAC), which will facilitate free movement of labour and goods among its members. This is important because while Africa's exports to the rest of the world are often focused around a few primary commodities, intra-African trade is more evenly distributed among fuels, non-fuel primary products and manufactured goods. As intra-regional trade grows, it can be expected that the range of exports will follow suit as well.

Notes

1. *Diversification: Towards A New Paradigm for Africa's Development;* H. Ben Hammouda, S.N. Karingi, A.E. Njuguna and M. Sadni-Jallab, 2006a. And *Accelerating Africa's Development through Diversification;* UNECA Economic Report on Africa 2007; *www.uneca.org/era2007.*

2. Of crucial relevance for regional economic integration and diversification is the facilitation of the movements of labour, capital and goods and services.

3. The UNECA study found that greater diversification in an economy leads to higher total productivity of both labour and capital (see pp. 144-145).

4. These issues were explored in previous reports of UN-OSAA, i.e. "The Role of the Private Sector for the Implementation of the New Partnership for Africa's Development", UN-OSAA 2006; and "The Private Sector's Institutionalised Response to NEPAD: A Review of Current Experience and Practices" UN-OSAA 2007.

5. For example, see: UNECA. "The 2007 Big Table: Managing Africa's Natural Resources for Growth and Poverty Reduction", *op. cit.*

6. These aspects of trade flows were among the key points stressed in the Expert Group Meeting on Economic Diversification in Africa organised by UNOSAA, held in Addis Ababa on 17-18 November 2009.

7. This is linked to overall interest in regional integration and institutions since 1945 and reflected in the establishment of such bodies as the EU, ASEAN and UN institutions as well as African regional bodies, which have received special note in the UN Charter.

8. *Building Bridges: China's Growing Role as Infrastructure Financier for Sub-Saharan Africa;* V. Foster, W. Butterfield, C. Chen and N. Pushak; World Bank, 2008.

9. See Mobile Telecommunications press release, 11 March 2009: *http://mtechzambia. com/Press%20Release%20110309.pdf.*

10. J. Imbs and R. Wacziarg (2003), Stages of Diversification, *American Economic Review*, 93(1), pp. 63-86.

11. IMF *World Economic Outlook Database*, October 2009.

12. OECD, *African Economic Outlook 2010;* p. 52.

Chapter 2

Experiences in National Economic Diversification in Africa

The five countries selected for this study are Angola, Benin, Kenya, South Africa and Tunisia, all of which can offer insights about diversification in Africa. Angola represents a country that is dependent on one main product, oil, to fuel its growth. So far, oil revenues have helped make Angola one of the fastest growing economies in the world, but it has also made the country vulnerable to boom-and-bust cycles due to fluctuations in oil prices.[1] The report will consider how Angola can wean itself from its oil dependency and develop a broader range of exports and revenue sources.

Kenya has made a great deal of progress in diversifying its economy and is poised to become an economic powerhouse in East Africa and even on the continent. Benin, on the other hand, has not been as successful in strengthening its economy and is hampered by its lack of lucrative natural resources. Strategies for Benin and countries with a similar profile will be analysed.

South Africa and Tunisia have more diversified and developed economies than most countries in Africa and act as hubs in their respective regional economies. The Report will look at how they have built such diverse economies and what lessons could be drawn from these experiences in the region.

2.1. South Africa case study

Economic background

The South African economy has long been the largest, and one of the most diversified, economies in Africa. Its GDP grew strongly after 2000, but began to decline in 2008 and even turned negative in 2009, at the height of the global financial crisis (Figure 2.1). Manufacturing dropped, mining activities slumped and agriculture was badly hit. The automotive sector, a big contributor to international trade tax revenues, also saw output decline massively. In fact, only the construction sector was sparred because of the works associated with the 2010 Football World Cup. The consequences of the crisis highlighted South Africa's strong integration with the global economy, and the vulnerabilities that can result thereof.

Figure 2.1. **South Africa's GDP growth**

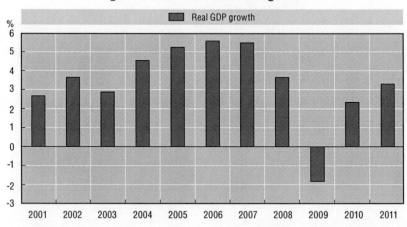

South Africa's economic success[2] is based in part on its extraordinary mineral wealth. However, a continued over-reliance on commodity-based sectors and heavy industry exposes the country to problems associated with insufficient diversification. Despite a number of new initiatives to diversify the economy, there is ongoing reliance on traditional sectors.[3] South Africa has a well-established manufacturing base, which was developed in the early twentieth century and is strongly linked to traditional sectors such as agriculture and mining. In general, this manufacturing base is a key driver of economic growth and diversification. This is illustrated by the presence of industries such as agro-processing, metals and leather, as well as construction and engineering specifically geared for mining, geological projects, and financial services that also often specialise in local sectors. In recent years, new sectors have opened up, such as the automobile industry and call centres, sometimes with strong government support. Tourism is seen as an important component of the country's economic development, because of its spill-over effects in developing infrastructure (roads and airports especially), construction of hotels and other facilities, job creation and image-building for the country as a whole. Figure 2.2 illustrates the composition of South Africa's diverse economy.

Figure 2.2. **Composition of South Africa's GDP 2008**

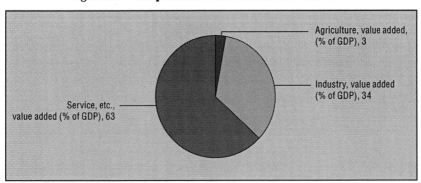

The South African economy is quite competitive – ranked 45th out of 133 in the 2009 Global Competitiveness Index. It is the second most competitive country on the continent after Tunisia. According to the same Index, it tops the list in financial market and business sophistication, technological readiness, market size, and performs very well in innovation.[4] These are all strengths that support South Africa's well-diversified economy. Its financial sector, for example, ensures easy access to credit and this in turn fuels the growth of business and enterprise, key engines of economic growth and innovation.

However, South Africa also needs to overcome some of the binding constraints to its growth. High unemployment rates have been attributed in part to the decline in the tradable sectors, especially manufacturing, which use low-skilled labour intensively (Dube, Hausmann, and Rodrik, 2007). The high compensation costs for managerial and professional staff also weaken South Africa's competitiveness and undercut the profits of foreign investors. To address the skills shortage, South Africa needs to strengthen higher education and training, ensure a more flexible labour market and smooth employer-worker relations. This would all help to improve labour market efficiency, in which South Africa does not perform well.

On the positive side, initiatives taken in new fields, such as automobiles, have proved to be successful. The same applies to the emphasis given to supporting diversified economic growth in neighbouring countries that have strong ties to South Africa's economy,[5] and to exploring the way in which international linkages such as with Brazil, India and China could help promote diversified economic growth. Also, South Africa's traditionally strong public service sector has played a major role in carrying economic growth in the national economy, allowing it to have a favourable effect on the region. But as the economy continues to develop, capacity to support this growth will have to be strengthened to reap development benefits.

Role of government

In the 1950s and 1960s, the South African Government established entities such as Phoskor to produce phosphates urgently needed for agriculture, and SASOL to spearhead oil produced through a liquefaction process from coal, to offset South Africa's dependence on imported oil. SASOL, a largely privatised company, is one of the world's largest oil-from-coal enterprises and one of Africa's largest corporations. The Government also established the Industrial Development Corporation (IDC) to provide finance for strategic enterprises which lack commercial funding but have the potential to drive economic diversification activities.

Many institutions created before the 1990s have continued to stimulate South Africa's economic diversification during the post-1994 period, and new entities and programmes have emerged (Box 2.1). Examples of government

---

Box 2.1. **Promoting industrial development in South Africa: The Industrial Development Corporation**

South Africa's Industrial Development Corporation, a state-owned development finance institution, has been active for the past sixty years to promote new industrial enterprises and undertakings in South Africa. It is active in developing employment-generating activities in rural areas, financing and supporting SMEs, nurturing technology-based organisations; promoting investment in industrial development zones; facilitating large beneficiation projects that support manufacturing activities; and providing credit facilities to South African exporters and importers. As part of its industrial promotion mandate, it offers a wide range of financial options – equity, venture capital, commercial debt and so on to enterprises in non-traditional sectors such as chemicals, media and motion pictures and franchising. It is also active beyond South Africa's borders. The IDC was, for example, a key player in the MOZAL aluminium plant in Mozambique.

Source: Industrial Development Corporation of South Africa, 2010.

---

institutions whose actions support economic diversification both inside South Africa and increasingly in Africa include the South African Bureau of Standards (SABS) and the Council for Scientific and Industrial Research (CSIR). As for other Government initiatives, the Development Fund of the South African Foreign Ministry has become the African Renaissance Fund since 1994 and is aimed at supporting various projects in bi- or trilateral partnerships that are often related to economic diversification.

A major step taken by government in 2007 was the creation of the National Industrial Policy Framework (NIPF) and its Industrial Policy Action Plan (IPAP). One of the IPAP's goals is to "facilitate diversification beyond [South Africa's] current reliance on traditional commodities and non-tradable services. This requires the promotion of increased value-addition characterised particularly by movement into non-traditional tradable goods and services that compete in export markets as well as against imports".[6] The IPAP identified a number of sectors in its drive to meet this objective, and they have been organised around three clusters:[7]

- **Cluster 1 – Qualitatively new areas of focus:**
  - ❖ realising the potential of the metal fabrication, capital and transport equipment sectors, particularly arising from large public investments;
  - ❖ "green" and energy-saving industries;
  - ❖ agro-processing, linked to food security and food pricing imperatives.
- **Cluster 2 – Scale up and broaden interventions in existing IPAP sectors:**
  - ❖ automotives, components, medium and heavy commercial vehicles;
  - ❖ plastics, pharmaceuticals and chemicals;
  - ❖ clothing, textiles, footwear and leather;
  - ❖ bio fuels;
  - ❖ forestry, paper, pulp and furniture;
  - ❖ strengthening linkages between cultural industries and tourism;
  - ❖ business process servicing.
- **Cluster 3 – Sectors with potential for long-term advanced capabilities:**
  - ❖ nuclear;
  - ❖ advanced materials;
  - ❖ aerospace.

For each of these sectors, the IPAP outlines a sector profile; key opportunities; major constraints; and key action programmes, outcomes, and milestones for developing the sector. The IPAP is certainly exemplary, and illustrates one way in which government action can help to boost diversification by promoting strategic sectors of the economy.

In addition to the IPAP and in support of the NIPF, the Department of Trade and Industry (DTI) initiated a Regional Industrial Development Strategy (RIDS) that proposed state intervention to address regional disparities inside South Africa. At the same time, the IPAP was slated to have cross-cutting actions that included the targeting of industrial financing, the enhancement of innovation and technology, intellectual property protection, and reducing input costs through competition policy.

There is also the Motor Industry Development Program (MIDP), which was launched in 1995 to boost South Africa's promising automobile assembly industry. A number of examples illustrate the success of this programme: in 2002 BMW's plant near Pretoria, which produced cars for global export markets, won the prize for the best BMW factory in Europe/Africa; in 2005 General Motors invested USD 3 billion in South Africa to manufacture the Hummer H3 for export to Asia, the Middle East, Africa and Europe; in 2006, Volkswagen announced plans to invest USD 3.7 billion to produce Golf 5 cars for export to Asia and Australasia; and in 2007, Daimler-Chrysler decided to produce its new C-class Sedans in South Africa.

Other government-led initiatives on economic development undertaken in the post-1994 period have helped to boost diversification in South Africa.[8] However, there have also been criticisms of certain government policies. Despite the successes in the motor industry, some analysts have argued that the IPAP sectors are not the most promising for the future of South Africa's economy. Some economists consider that the South African Government has been targeting industries that would not be sustainable without protection and should instead focus on resource-based sectors that enable South Africa to be internationally competitive.[9]

Critics also bemoan the lack of action to build entrepreneurial and technical capacities through more co-operative mechanisms between the public and private sectors.[10] Moreover, the Government can do more in terms of improving infrastructure, given that demand has outpaced existing infrastructure capacities in recent years. This is especially relevant for the country's power sector. There has not been enough investment in new generation capacity and as a result, the country has been plagued by "load shedding" or power cuts. The recent creation of a National Planning Commission, however, has great potential for overcoming many shortcomings and giving government new relevance as a driver of diversification.

Private sector

The South African private sector is heavily involved in most of the key areas of the economy. Due to its size, complexity and links to major global corporations, it has played a major role in enabling South Africa to become an emerging economic powerhouse. Moreover, the growing involvement of South African economic interests in Africa, driven by private sector companies and parastatals, has helped South Africa become a dominant economic force in the continent. In this way, the private sector has often been South Africa's bridge to sub-Saharan Africa, the broader region and the international economy.

Infrastructure

South Africa has one of the most developed infrastructure systems in Africa (see Box 2.2). It is the only country with toll-road concessions, for example, and its local financial markets have been instrumental in funding infrastructure projects. Nevertheless, South Africa must still mobilise significant amounts of resources to meet the cost of its large needs for infrastructure development, rehabilitation and maintenance.[11] Most of the spending is needed for investment in electricity infrastructure. South Africa has enjoyed high economic growth rates but generation capacity in electricity has not kept pace with demand, which has grown much faster. The government's efforts to introduce private participation in the electricity sector, which had long been run by the state utility, Eskom, failed, in part because low tariffs for electricity were not attractive enough to profit-conscious private investors (AICD, 2009). As a result, South Africa has been experiencing a power crisis marked by blackouts and a slow-down in economic activity.

South Africa has played an important role in supporting the infrastructure systems of other countries on the continent. For example, it has contributed to the Pan African Infrastructure Development Fund, whose goal is to raise money to finance commercially-viable infrastructure projects in Africa. South Africa's mobile phone operators, such as Vodacom and MTN, are active in several African countries and have helped to support small businesses in areas that otherwise would not have had access to a phone network. Also, some of the most important transport corridors that are opening new opportunities for trade in the region run through South Africa: the Maputo Development Corridor from Johannesburg to Maputo in Mozambique; the Trans-Kalahari Corridor from Johannesburg to Walvis Bay in Namibia; and the so-called North-South corridor from Johannesburg to Burundi, as well as corridors from Johannesburg to South African coastal areas like Cape Town, Durban and Coega. In addition, Eskom supplies 70% of the region's electricity. This shows how the continental spread of South African economic interests has helped boost not only the South African economy but those of other regional economies as well.

Natural resources

The South African economy has long been driven by its massive mineral deposits. As of 2008, platinum was South Africa's number one export

---

Box 2.2. **South Africa's Approach to Developing Infrastructure**

The South African government has taken a number of measures to promote infrastructure, and thereby support economic activities. It has a well-developed Public Private Partnerships (PPP) framework that is institutionalised under a PPP law and a PPP Unit in the National Treasury. The PPP Unit offers technical assistance on PPP projects and plays a regulatory role by managing tenders, approving feasibility studies and providing guidance on the aspects of PPP projects. Within the course of eight years, the PPP Unit had completed 60 PPP projects, including the Gautrain, a rapid rail link between Johannesburg and Pretoria, the biggest PPP project in Africa. By promoting increased public-private co-operation in infrastructure development, South Africa's PPP policy has in turn helped to facilitate economic activities that are crucial for productivity and growth.

Another exemplary approach that South Africa has undertaken is in renewable energy. South Africa derives most of its energy from coal, but given the implications on the environment and climate change, as well as the power shortages the country has been experiencing, the government plans to diversify South Africa's energy sources away from coal. It set a target that 15% of its energy source must be from renewable sources by 2020. Also, the national regulator, NERSA, established feed-in tariffs for electricity from renewable energy sources. The tariffs – set at above-market rates and guaranteed for 20 years – are a way to attract private investment in this emerging sector.

The private sector has been very active in terms of financing projects and developing them. For example, the Bethlehem hydroelectric project in South Africa is the first hydropower project to be launched by an Independent Power Producer (IPP) in South Africa. More needs to be done, but these first efforts to boost the renewable energy sector may lead to skills-development as well as greater use of technology given the specific nature of renewable energy.

---

commodity, having long eclipsed gold and diamonds. Agriculture has slowly dropped in prominence but the Government used the food crisis of 2007-08 as an impetus for new measures to revitalise farming and regain agricultural self-sufficiency. However, the challenges of water scarcity in Southern Africa and often poor soil conditions remain considerable, and there is a great need for land-ownership reform as a way to expand agriculture.

In mining and agriculture, the state has continued to insist on the necessity for greater beneficiation of resources, but the vehicles for this roll-out, such as capacity building programmes in partnership with the private sector, are often missing.

South Africa's bio-diversity is a key factor underpinning its strong tourism sector. The state has announced its intentions to expand what is seen as a key sector for future employment creation. Interestingly, the state has devolved some control over tourism, as the recent moves to sell off state land to local communities for tourism ventures has demonstrated. Such moves are expected to expand the scope and size of tourism and to ensure its impact on a broad-based range of activities. The "Boundless Southern Africa" initiative of some Southern African Development Community (SADC) governments, which focuses on using trans-frontier national parks in the region as key driving factors for expanded regional tourism, has been largely initiated and driven by South Africa.[12]

Human resources

Compared to most African economies, South Africa has a well-developed labour force and strong human resources capacity. Yet it needs expansion in crucially important sectors such as engineering and in growing sectors such as information technology, services and new forms of energy. South Africa could, for example, become a leader in nuclear energy, but trained personnel are almost non-existent. The use of scarce skills in the most effective manner is therefore crucial, and the Government has introduced e-governance and e-training initiatives across a vast spectrum of sectors to do so.

Education is a key government priority, with a share of 20% of the national budget. This focus is important for addressing challenges such as illiteracy, which in 2008 stood at 12.2%. However, funds must be targeted more effectively in order to improve results and meet key development goals. This might involve better vocational training, increased funding for research centres, and scholarships for university students, especially for traditionally marginal sectors with a strong potential for growth.

Financial resources

The South African economy is fortunate to have possibly the best-developed financial sector in Africa, with a vast spectrum of international linkages to mobilise funds, as well as a well-developed domestic financial market with a broad range of services. This is of crucial importance in the context of the SADC regional economy and has been an asset to boost economic activities in the rest of Africa.

The South African economy is increasingly dominated by its services sector. Financial services are a key service area, and South Africa boasts some of the best banking regulations in the world. The financial sector was badly impacted by the global financial crisis, and the Johannesburg Securities Exchange (JSE) lost 26% in market value between July and November 2008 and portfolio flows decreased. However, compared to other countries South African banks were relatively unscathed because they had little exposure to the subprime market. The effect on the JSE was temporary too, and within a few months, portfolio flows picked up and credit spreads decreased – a testament to the resilience of the JSE (AEO, 2010).

Regional context

South Africa has one of the largest and most diverse economies in Africa. Because of its economic and political clout, many regional groupings are located there, including the Southern African Customs Union (SACU), which is made up of Botswana, Lesotho, Namibia, South Africa and Swaziland. Moreover, South Africa is a key member of the Southern African Development Community (SADC), which represents the most integrated and strongest regional economy in Africa.[13] SACU is a key facet of the broader economic regional context of SADC and can be used as a strong base for regional economic integration and diversification.[14]

South Africa's important position as a driver of economic development and diversification in Africa has been enhanced by its commercial reach across the continent and its integration in global supply chains, helping it to increasingly become an economic hub for SSA and a bridge to the global economy. In this context, South Africa's geo-strategic location, together with its resource wealth, has long attracted international political and economic interests.

Historically, Cape Town has been a key frontier town for international trade, a role it continues to play today given the rise of Asian traders in the world economy and their interest in Africa, as well as an increase in sea-borne trade passing through the Cape. South Africa's coastal locations have given it exposure to major international economic interests and have helped it to establish early diversification of the South African economy.

In spite of this important regional dynamic, there has been some uncertainty in South Africa's policy towards key regional bodies such as SACU, specifically regarding the possible expansion of SACU's scope and the continuation of the customs collection/distribution mechanism – which South Africa has controlled since SACU's inception – at SADC level.

SADC's plans to become a customs union could cast uncertainty over the current makeup and operations of SACU. In October 2008 SADC, COMESA and the EAC agreed to move towards becoming a tripartite free trade area (FTA) as an initial goal.[15] This plan has now overtaken initiatives looking at other more closely integrated mechanisms to merge the economies of Southern and Eastern Africa.

Such a move seems more practical than a customs union spanning these three RECs. Moreover, South Africa is the dominant economy in the region and tends to attract more economic activity than other countries in Southern Africa. It produced 71.7% of the GDP of SADC in 2004, with Angola and Tanzania, the second and third largest economies in the region, having a contribution of respectively 6.6 and 3.7%. Seven of the fourteen SADC member states contributed less than 2% to the region's GDP. In the SACU grouping South Africa is responsible for 99.3% of total SACU trade. Certainly, the diverse South African economy remains a stimulant for other economies within SADC but there can also be an adverse effect on neighbouring countries when South Africa's economy does not fare well.

The international context

The South African economy is heavily integrated with the global community, producing knock-on effects for its African economic partners. For example, South Africa's exposure to global crises can amplify recessionary tendencies among its neighbours; by the same token, positive growth in South Africa can boost the economies of its neighbours.

South Africa has a significant economic partnership with the EU. It is South Africa's major trading partner, source of FDI and development partner. South Africa has preferential economic and trade agreements with the EU and the USA and is currently negotiating free trade deals with India, Mercosur (South America's primary trading bloc) and China.

The existing trade relations with the EU have been undertaken through a Trade, Development and Co-operation Agreement (TDCA) since 2000. This was Africa's first WTO-compatible Free Trade Agreement (FTA) with any country, and was perceived as being a stimulant to economic diversification and as contributing to helping South Africa to compete in the open international economy.

At the same time, the Economic Partnership Agreements (EPAs) between the EU and Regional Economic Communities (RECs) are meant to promote diversified economic development and regional economic integration in Africa through mutually advantageous commercial relations. However, the fact that the EPAs must be WTO-compatible presents a challenge for Africa, even if compliance could improve Africa's capacity to cope in the new global economy (a factor that encouraged the Caribbean group of countries to conclude a full EPA with the EU in 2008).

The SADC EPA was supposed to harmonise the trade aspects of the TDCA with those of the rest of SACU, Mozambique and Angola. In 2006 the other members of SACU wanted South Africa's trade regime *vis-à-vis* the EU to be included within the SADC EPA so as to strengthen regional integration and the regional economy of Southern Africa using the strong economic ties with the EU. It was thought that this would create an improved investment climate for the SACU region and ultimately SADC, thereby allowing SACU to better access new opportunities that would also support diversification for the bloc.[16]

South Africa did not agree to certain issues such as services and the Most Favoured Nation (MFN) reciprocity proposed by the EU, and withdrew from initiating the Interim EPA (IEPA) with other countries in 2007. In 2009, the other members of SACU apart from Namibia signed the IEPA along with Mozambique. It is possible that some formulae can be found in 2010 to allow South Africa either to join the Final EPA or to harmonise its TDCA-based trading relationship with the EU with those of the other regional countries vis-à-vis the EU. If this is done, it could be a stimulus to the regional economy which may lead to further diversification.[17] Provided Namibia's abstention can be resolved, the EPA framework can be given a chance to help strengthen an integrated regional economy. A key challenge will be for the EU to expand access in agri-products from the entire region.

China has thus far not been a major investor in South African infrastructure or resources compared to its investment in other countries in the region. By 2008, China had invested in just five mining projects in South Africa (mostly in chrome), with little investment in infrastructure. However, China has been active in other ways in the South African economy – its new China African Development (CAD) Fund, for example, is located in South Africa. More generally, China's investments in other countries in the region help develop new opportunities for the South African economy and help South Africa to form linkages with other emerging economies.

Indeed, new diplomatic initiatives such as those vis-à-vis China, India and Brazil have established new partnerships with great potential in addition to South Africa's long-standing economic relationships. South Africa has placed great emphasis on an expanding relationship with these countries. Through the India-Brazil-South Africa (IBSA) trilateral dialogue process, South Africa takes advantage of its South-South partnership to boost trade, tourism, agriculture, science and technology and a host of other economic areas.

In order to best utilise opportunities for diversified economic growth, South Africa needs to build on these diplomacy efforts. This is especially important given its membership in many overlapping institutions in Africa and internationally.

2.2. Kenya case study

Economic background

The Kenyan economy has long been one of the most diversified in Africa. Kenya's economy is based on traditional sectors such as agriculture and tourism but to better insulate its economy from economic crises, it needs further diversification. For example, the political turbulence in 2008 badly affected Kenya's tourism, at a time when agricultural growth was slowing down. Drought and worries about food security are ongoing challenges facing the Kenyan economy. However, Kenya's strong private sector has helped to lay a foundation for stronger growth in services, which have been largely driven by traditional sectors and Kenya's important geo-strategic location.

Tourism and agriculture are the traditional pillars of Kenya's economy. The former has been one of the strongest sectors with the greatest potential for further growth. In agriculture, tea is Kenya's top commodity. There has been tremendous growth in horticulture, although there have been limitations to expanding both tea production and horticulture because of long distances to markets and high air freight costs. The services sector has also been quite strong. Kenya's strategic location between the Indian Ocean and the regional hinterland affords it many opportunities for trade and investment, although this location's usefulness depends also on a good transportation network. Ongoing problems related to infrastructure are especially pronounced, particularly in respect to the crucially important transportation and energy sectors.

As Table 2.1 illustrates, Kenya has been enjoying solid GDP growth, although it was not impervious to the economic crisis and saw a dip in growth in 2008/09. Similarly, trade levels were badly affected, although projections show a rebound over the next couple of years.

Table 2.1. **Kenya: Selected economic/trade indicators, 2006-12**
Annual percentage change, unless otherwise indicated

Nominal accounts and prices	2006/07	2007/08	2008/09 (est.)	2009/10 (est.)	2010/11 (proj.)	2011/12 (proj.)
Real GDP growth (market prices)	6.7	4.3	2.2	3.2	4.6	5.5
Real GDP per capita	4.1	1.7	0.0	1.4	2.8	3.7
Import volume growth, goods and services	9.3	6.4	7.8	5.1	2.1	7.1
Import value growth, goods and services	22.3	23.4	3.9	−3.3	8.5	10.6
Export volume growth, goods and services	5.5	10.7	4.0	2.9	7.5	8.3
Export value growth, goods and services	19.9	1.8	−3.0	11.5	12.5	14.7
Terms of trade, goods and services	−2.3	−9.2	−0.3	2.8	−4.3	−0.3

Source: IMF Article IV Consultation, 2010.

Kenya is taking notable steps to build on its existing capacities to help drive economic diversification within an integrated regional economy. The region provides a favourable context and much is being done by all stakeholders to take matters forward in the EAC and other regional institutions, including the Economic Community of the Great Lakes Countries (ECGLC) and the Great Lakes Parliamentary Forum on Peace. The East African Community recently launched its common market framework, which will allow for the easy movement of goods, labour and services. Kenya can take advantage of these regional set-ups to benefit its economy, and, in turn, to contribute to the regional economy.

Geographically, Kenya is well-positioned on the Indian Ocean, facing Asia and with access to key shipping lanes between the Mediterranean and Indian Oceans. This geographic advantage has been a basis of the overall strategies of the Kenyan Government in working towards greater diversification of its economy; together with a willingness to seize international opportunities (see Box 2.3 as an example).

Box 2.3. **Boosting telecommunications in Kenya**

Seacom is a 17 000 km under-water fibre optic cable that links south and east Africa to global networks via India and Europe. The implications of the project are huge: the expansion of broadband services; a chance for local industries to be connected to international customers; and support for service-provision in education, health and other public sectors. It will boost science and research in the region, and will make recipient countries competitive as ICT hubs, especially compared to emerging countries like India. By lowering the costs of telecommunications, the Seacom cable offers the chance for more Africans to get connected to phone and internet technologies. Moreover, Seacom is 75% African-owned and is an important example of regional co-operation to boost technologies and reap economies of scale. Kenya hosts a submarine terminal station for Seacom, and has undertaken a similar project, the East African Marine Cable (TEAMS) to connect Kenya to the United Arab Emirates. Kenya plans to take advantage of both Seacom and TEAMS to boost its business process outsourcing and call-centre businesses, both fledgling but highly promising activities.

Kenya has had laudable success in terms of expanding diversification, including in the horticultural sector, which grew fourfold since 1974 to become Kenya's third largest source of foreign exchange after tourism and tea by 2006. Other results include the diversification of financial services and the development of information technologies, both important contributors to Kenya's national economy and that of the region. Kenya's success has been especially noteworthy given the challenging regional context and the recent political turbulence.

The East African regional economy in which Kenya operates is relatively strong, diversified and well-integrated, and promotes stability and growth not only in the immediate region but in SSA and the Indian Oceanic region. East

Africa as a region includes three large states – Kenya, Tanzania and Uganda – that are relatively well-balanced in terms of their size and population, and whose economies can profit from regional integration.Regional co-ordination is particularly important in light of shared access to Lake Victoria and for the land-locked countries.

The regional context provides opportunities for the expanding sectors in Kenya, and most importantly for its service sector. As the Kenyan economy has become a business hub for the increasingly integrated East African region, services are expected to grow.

A variety of initiatives that help develop a strong integrated East African economy are endorsed and facilitated by the Kenyan Government, although in many cases the powerful Kenyan private sector has been a major initiator as well. These include the creation of a regional stock exchange, regional harmonisation of transportation standards and procedures, and the standardisation of academic qualifications for regional institutions. In most instances, Nairobi has been the geographical focal point for such activities.

Role of government

Traditionally the Kenyan public service has been relatively well developed, with solid policies and regulatory frameworks.

For instance, the Kenyan Government directed targeted support to the horticulture sector, to the extent than Kenya's flower exports have surpassed the traditional leading crops of tea and coffee. In 2006, horticulture was the third largest source of foreign exchange earnings in the Kenyan economy after tourism and tea. While the private sector has played an active role in this development, government guidance, support and strategies, including those involving export market destinations and making sure exports meet market criteria, also played an instrumental role. Kenya's Horticultural Crop Development Agency (HCDA) has been the main institution involved, facilitating sector network rather than exercising direct control.

Among the various government initiatives to spearhead diversification in the economy, the principal one is Vision 2030, the government's key policy for Kenya's economic development in the years leading to 2030. Vision 2030 identifies economic diversification as the main thrust of this development strategy. Moreover, the Kenyan Government has indicated that an appropriate policy directed at diversifying the national economy for its production and exports has been the core of the Government's Economic Recovery Strategy (ERS) and is the main underlying rationale for Vision 2030.[18] At the core of Vision 2030 is Nairobi Metro 2030, a blueprint to make Nairobi a world-class African city for business and residence. The two could help to boost Kenya's standing as a national economic powerhouse, with a vibrant and promising capital city.

Private sector

The Kenyan private sector is well developed and has engaged in dialogue with the Government on an ongoing basis. An example of public/private co-operation and consultancy in support of government initiatives is the strong private sector presence on the National Economic and Social Council (NESC) linked to the office of the Presidency, which appraises the effectiveness of government policies. The Kenya Private Sector Alliance has been especially active in engaging with government to create a stable environment to support business development in Kenya, helping set goals such as those included in the National Business Agenda. Moves towards improved regional integration have often been initiated and driven by the private sector, which has worked with government for the adoption and implementation of such measures. Private sector initiatives are receiving support from government, for example through venture funds in support of developing entrepreneurs in ICT. Moreover, the success of horticulture in Kenya was partly the result of the private sector's partnership with the Government.

All the same, as Table 2.2 shows, in many respects Kenyan firms find it more difficult than their regional peers to access finance. This is an area that will need to be strengthened if Kenyan enterprises are to continue contributing significantly to economic activities in the country.

Table 2.2. **Access to finance for firms in Kenya**

Finance	Macro dimension			Micro dimension						
	Kenya	Region	Income	Small	Medium	Large	Exporter	Nonexporter	Domestic	Foreign
Firms with lines of credit or loans from financial institutions (%)	25.4	26.1	14.8	17.6	30.7	63.6	58.7	22.8	24.8	33.1
Internal finance for investment (%)	78.4	73.5	85.4	83.1	74.6	66.5	58.8	80.0	79.6	65.9
Bank finance for investment (%)	15.5	19.8	7.0	11.7	16.1	31.2	35.4	13.9	14.5	26.2
Owners' contribution, new equity shares (%)	0.1	0.2	0.5	0.1	0.1	0.1	0.2	0.1	0.1	0.2
Informal finance for investment (%)	2.2	3.1	4.6	2.8	2.0	0.1	1.6	2.3	2.4	0.3
Suppliers/customers credit financing (%)	17.0	19.7	15.1	13.7	21.9	25.1	30.6	15.9	16.3	24.6
Loans requiring collateral (%)	86.1	73.2	79.6	85.9	92.6	78.2	77.1	87.9	86.1	86.0
Values of collateral needed for a loan (% of the loan amount)	120.8	109.0	135.4	114.5	125.4	125.3	124.0	120.2	121.3	117.1
Firms with annual financial statement reviewed by external auditor (%)	49.5	60.4	33.0	33.6	73.1	92.3	93.3	46.1	46.2	91.3

Infrastructure

Existing transport corridors are being revamped with government support. One prominent example is the transport corridor from Mombasa to Uganda and eventually to Rwanda and the DRC. Government red-tape seems to be a major barrier to progress. The Government's key initiative, Vision 2030, has been largely built around the Mombasa/Nairobi corridor and now includes a new far northern corridor from Lamu on the north Kenyan coast into Sudan and Ethiopia.

Vision 2030 has also capitalised on the Kenyan position vis-à-vis the Southern Corridor from Dar es Salaam to Burundi, largely running through Tanzania, in its plans for the Kenyan/Tanzanian border area.

Natural resources

Kenya's natural resources include bio-diversity and natural attractions that support one of the most sophisticated tourism industries in Africa, as well as strong scientific and environmental activities to support these industries. Moreover, the richness of its soil has long supported a strong agricultural sector.

The Government has been active in managing these resources and has increasingly found ways to link them to related services. These initiatives often have a regional dimension, as in the co-ordination with Tanzania regarding eco-tourism in the Masai-Mara/Serengeti region. Vision 2030 explicitly calls for a regional dimension in eco-tourism, ranging from improved development of tourism in the trans-border region with Tanzania in the area of Amboseli, to strengthening Nairobi as a regional tourism services centre with eco-tourism being of central importance.

Human resources

Kenya has a high level of human resources, especially compared to other African countries. Literacy stands at about 88%, for example. There are ongoing programmes by the public and private sectors to support capacity building in specific sectors such as tourism. Kenya has high-quality scientific research institutions, invests strongly in research and development, and enjoys a significant level of collaboration between business and universities in research. These efforts are supported by the Government and link into economic blueprints for a more diversified economy. Growth strategies have been linked with human resource development in a variety of ways since independence in 1963. Agricultural settlement schemes and government intervention in business are examples that were also linked to diversification, such as initial steps in horticulture.

Regional institutions

Kenya is linked to its neighbours Uganda and Tanzania by their littoral positions around Lake Victoria. These countries have institutionalised their regional relationship through the East African Community (EAC), and Rwanda and Burundi have subsequently joined. The EAC acts as a facilitating platform for various forms of regional integration that promote Kenya's economic diversification. The transformation of the EAC into a full common market in November 2009 was a major step forward for East African economic integration and a strengthened, diversified regional economy.

A customs union, which is part of the EAC process, was launched in 2005 with its roll-out continuing according to plan. However, the overlapping membership of countries with EAC, COMESA and SADC[19] is a key problem which is acknowledged by EAC countries and also receiving attention in the AU process of Rationalisation of Regional Economic Communities. The overlap offers challenges on many fronts as it can lead to potentially conflicting integration processes. Tanzania for example is part of both the SADC customs union initiative and that of the EAC. The 2008 initiative to turn the regions covered by COMESA, the EAC and SADC into one Free Trade Area (FTA) could potentially overcome this problem. In the EAC process, the EAC members have committed themselves to the highest levels of integration including political federation.

The regional context is therefore a key dimension of the overall strategy of the Kenyan government in working towards greater diversification of its economy, in parallel with a willingness to utilise international opportunities.

The international context

Kenya is a leading country in the region in its dealings with the EU, China and other key development partners. Its strong relations have a major impact on economic diversification both for itself and for the region. Kenya is located on the Indian Ocean and has a transportation network that links much of the EAC and Intergovernmental Authority on Development (IGAD) regions with the coast and major sea routes across the Indian Ocean, and in turn the Pacific and the Mediterranean. The Kenyan Government has also emphasised good relations with other Indian Ocean littoral countries in the Gulf, among others.

The EU has been able to initial an Interim EPA with the EAC. The agreement could serve to strengthen diversification by focusing on critical sectors such as agriculture and services provided that the development component is included and implemented.

As for other economic partners, Chinese investment in Kenya has been increasing, although it is not as significant as in other, resource-rich African countries. The investments have mainly targeted infrastructure development, with important positive spill-over effects for other economic areas, and in support of regional integration.

2.3. Tunisia case study

Economic background

Despite the failures of political governance that have culminated in the fall of Ben Ali's regime, Tunisia has become a middle-income country with a relatively diverse economy (Figure 2.3). Since the late 1980s, Tunisia has undertaken macro-economic policies and structural reforms designed to transform the country into a market-driven economy with a liberalised trade regime. The reforms have borne fruit: GDP averaged 5% between 1999 and 2009, while inflation remained stable at 3%; the public debt-to-GDP ratio declined by 9 percentage points; and reserves more than doubled from 2 to 5 months of imports.[20] With US 3.597 in 2009, Tunisia has one of the highest GDP per capita in Africa. In addition, 95.5% of the population have access to health services and sector spending stood at 8.6% of the national budget in 2009.[21] Life expectancy rose to 74 years in 2008, up from 68 years in 1987, while infant mortality has fallen to 18% and fertility rates have fallen to 1.70%.[22]

Figure 2.3. **Tunisia's diverse economy**

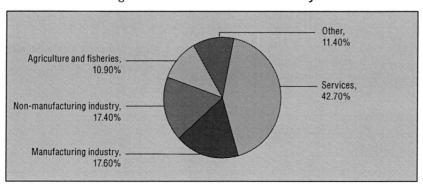

Tunisia has a number of comparative advantages that have helped it to develop a diverse economy, including its geographic location allowing for easy access to the European, Middle Eastern and African markets and enabling its companies to link into EU supply chains.

Despite the scarcity of natural resources, Tunisia has relied largely on a good business climate, infrastructure, geo-strategic location and highly skilled human resources to drive economic diversification. This has helped to make the economy more resilient to internal and external shocks, such as the surge in energy prices in 2008 and downturns in agriculture caused by drought. Moreover, its tourism sector is now being further developed to be a regional hub through new ventures such as health care, well being and sporting centres underpinned by massive investments from some Gulf countries. Also, services and manufacturing have recently been significantly enhanced to further increase Tunisia's economic diversification. For example, the establishment of more than 120 industrial zones and 10 techno-parks has helped to attract new Foreign Direct Investment (FDI).

Tunisia has taken advantage of its proximity to Europe to create an economic programme that is geared towards integration with the EU economy. For example, 72% of Tunisia's exports and 69% of its imports are with the EU (European Commission, 2008). Also, Tunisia has focused on short-orders from the EU in sectors such as textiles and garments for EU retail networks.[23] Such a process is now underway in several sectors ranging from automotive and electrical engineering to ICT and aeronautics, with Mercedes and recently Airbus making big investments in Tunisia.[24]

Tunisia's strengths in tourism, agriculture and ICT/services could be a major boost for the overall development of the North African economy.

Early this century, Tunisia identified four industrial sectors as priorities and each is already exporting more than EUR 1 billion worth of products: aeronautical and automotive components; ICT/off shoring; textile, leather and shoes; and food processing. These newly developing sectors are rapidly evolving towards becoming platforms for further diversified growth. The government also established capacity building programmes across all sectors and tourism, which is well-suited to Tunisia's circumstances.

Tunisia is the top performer in Africa and the 35th ranked in the world in terms of competitiveness, according to the 2011 World Competitiveness Report. It is more competitive than a number of EU member states such as Poland, Italy and Greece and also ahead of major emerging economies such as Brazil and India. Figure 2.4 shows a snapshot of Tunisia's competitiveness on a host of indicators. Its relatively small market size increases the importance of further regional integration.

Tunisia's trade policies have also helped it to become more competitive in international markets. It signed an association agreement with the EU in 1995, which set a deadline of 2008 for the removal of trade barriers for industrial goods, with ongoing negotiations for the service and agriculture sectors. In addition, Tunisia became the first country in the Mediterranean area to enter in a free trade area with the EU. It is also undertaking an Upgrading Program which aims to make Tunisian private sector enterprises globally competitive and includes training and infrastructure upgrading among other things. In light of these achievements, many West African governments are sending

Figure 2.4. **Indicators of Tunisia's competitiveness**

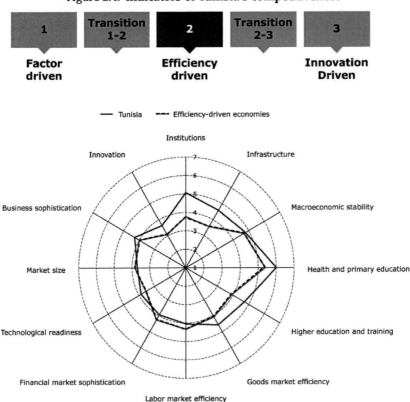

Source: *World Competitiveness Report 2010*, Country Profiles.

delegations to Tunisia to look at how to replicate such programmes in their own countries.

Role of government

Government programs and policies have played an important role in Tunisia's economic development. In the context of the Upgrading Program, various government agencies have given advice as well as mentorship – for a three year period – and substantial funding to companies. The country's priorities are reflected in the 11th National Development Plan, as described in Box 2.4.

The government's strategy has been to integrate Tunisia into the EU supply chain to make it a trade/services hub in the Mediterranean. A national strategy to make Tunisia a "Euro-Med Hub for Innovation" was designed for the period 2007-2016. This strategy of international economic integration supported by a range of policy measures, the most important being the establishment of an offshore regime for export-oriented and foreign-owned companies, has started

---

Box 2.4. Tunisia's 11th National Development Plan

- Economic growth target of 6% a year.

- Decrease unemployment from 13.9% in 2006 to 10-11% in 2011.

- Services, especially ICT, identified as strategic area.

- Increase value-addition in exports.

- Promote private initiatives and new partnerships to boost non-traditional, promising sectors such as agro-industry and chemical and bio-chemical industries.

- Increase agricultural production for products that have not yet met EU quotas.

- Reduce economic and social disparities by boosting regional development through technological centres, promotion of investments, and social actions.

---

to pay off and the new government should sustain the efforts aimed at further diversifying the economy into new sectors such as chemicals, bio-chemicals, engineering and electrical industries. Well-established sectors could also benefit from these diversification efforts, including the textiles sector, which should target a move from subcontracting to joint-contracting and to public tender. A major source of new jobs is expected to come from a further expansion of the service sector and in particular from tourism, ICT and business process outsourcing services.

Private sector

A long-established, growing, and well educated middle class is a key backbone of the Tunisian economy. The private sector is well developed and in 2009, private investment accounted for 60.3% of total investment[25] and the new Investment Promotion Code, including the "Concessions Act" as well as "Economic Initiative Act", should increase this contribution since private companies will be allowed to invest in public infrastructure and amenities through public-private partnerships (PPPs).

Infrastructure

The existing transport infrastructure, already quite extensive in domestic and international linkages, is being upgraded. The upgrade includes a number of projects such as the newly opened International Airport at Enfidha, the country's ninth airport, with an overall capacity of 7 million passengers in its first phase. An open-skies agreement has recently been signed with the EU and the tender for a deep-sea port at Enfidha, the first of its kind and the eighth in the country, is also planned for 2011. In addition, there is ongoing development of much needed new SDI/SDP coastal transportation networks that will help integrate the Tunisian economy with its neighbours in the North African region. Tunisia owns an extensive network of 20 000 kilometres in paved roads and 360 kilometres of freeways, and the country's stretch of the Trans-Maghreb highway link is about to reach the Algerian border. In addition, the country's railway network is 2 167 kilometres long and other projects are in progress, including the electrification of the Tunis-Borj Cedria line and the Réseau Ferroviaire Rapide (RFR) project. Overall, it has a well-developed infrastructure sector (see Table 2.3) which gives a major boost to other economic activities.

Table 2.3. **Tunisia's infrastructure sectors**
■ Competitive advantage   ● Competitive disadvantage

Indicator	Rank/133	
2nd pillar: Infrastructure		●
2.01 Quality of overall infrastructure	35	■
2.02 Quality of roads	39	■
2.03 Quality of railroad infrastructure	28	■
2.04 Quality of port infrastructure	41	■
2.05 Quality of air transport infrastructure	30	■
2.06 Available seat kilometres[1]	71	■
2.07 Quality of electricity supply	34	■
2.08 Telephones lines[1]	81	■

1. Hard data.
Source: *Africa Competitiveness Report 2009*, Tunisia country profile.

Natural resources

In spite of its relatively limited amount of good soil, Tunisia has been able to develop a strong agricultural sector. It relies on a relatively small number of products but has been able to diversify into a variety of agri-business activities. Moreover, Tunisia has used its scenic landscape and coast to develop one of the leading tourism sectors on the North African coastline. Also, it has made use of its abundant solar energy to develop renewable energy domestically, notably through the Tunisian Solar Plan (TSP), which was launched in 2009 and is comprised of 40 projects aiming to increase domestic production of renewable energy by 550 MW within five years.[26] Tunisia is also part of international initiatives like DESERTEC, a multi-country project to build several solar power stations in the Sahara desert for export in the region and in Europe.[27] In fact, Tunisia will host the DESERTEC University Network, a scientific research institution aimed at promoting desert technologies. Based in Tunis, it will bring together several countries from Europe and the MENA region. This Network will contribute to other efforts to boost Tunisia's science profile and is an example of how natural resources can be exploited for economic growth and diversification.

Human resources

Tunisia has a strong human resource base, including a well trained and motivated labour force which has been supported by government initiatives and by private sector collaboration. Indeed, Tunisia is ranked 7th out of 133 countries in terms of the quality of its Maths and Science education and in the top 20 in the quality of its education system overall (*World Competitiveness Report* 2009). The enrolment rates for children at the age of 6 reached 99% in 2006-07 (for both sexes) and the budget of the Ministry of Education and Training represented 16.93% of the state budget in 2007 and 22% in 2009. With 360 172 students enrolled in higher education programmes in 2009, 59.5% of whom were women, and with the full adoption of the European model for higher education by 2011, Tunisia is making strides to reinforce its excellent human resource base, which serves as a key pillar of the country's economic growth.

Financial resources

Tunisia's financial sector remained fairly robust during the global financial crisis due to excess liquidity and limited exposure to global markets. Today the banking landscape includes 20 commercial banks, with 11 publicly traded on the Tunis Stock Exchange. However the banking sector is expected to consolidate in the coming years as the number of banks is considered to be large compared with a national population of 10.4 million. In addition, a number of Tunisian banks have set their sights on regional expansion and need therefore to reach a critical size to be better placed for this endeavour. The construction of the Tunis Financial Harbour, the first off-shoring centre in North Africa, started in June 2009. The Tunisian Bourse des Valeurs Mobilières (BVMT) experienced a strong performance at the onset of the financial crisis – up 48% at the end of 2008 – and was the only Arab stock exchange to close in positive territory. Tunisia's insurance sector registered EUR 507.2 m in premium income in 2008 and the market is rising steadily due to an affluent, educated population and strong competition among the 23 active insurance firms. However, several challenges to doing business remain. Enterprises rank access to finance as the second biggest obstacle to doing business,[28] and indeed Tunisia's financial sector does not offer a comparative advantage compared to others (Table 2.4). If Tunisia is to expand its economic base, the lack of depth in the financial sector is an issue that will need to be addressed.

Table 2.4. **Tunisia's financial sector**

■ Competitive advantage   ● Competitive disadvantage

Indicator	Rank/133	
8th pillar: Financial market sophistication		●
Financial market sophistication	72	■
Financing through local equity market	43	■
Ease of access to loans	56	■
Venture capital availability	36	■
Restriction on capital flows	89	■
Strength of investor protection[1]	110	■
Soundness of banks	76	■
Regulation of securities exchanges	43	■
Legal rights index[1]	98	■

1. Hard data.
Source: Africa Competitiveness Report 2009, Tunisia country profile.

Regional and international institutions

Although hampered by the lack of strong inter-governmental cooperation, the Arab Maghreb Union (AMU) is a potentially important regional institution. Currently, Tunisia is a key participant in two of AMU's projects which have the potential to profoundly strengthen North-Africa's diversification and the integration of the regional and national economies. The first project is an improved transport system with highway construction and parallel rail developments, including the use of high-speed trains along the North African coastline. The second project is a regional bank, funded by all AMU members, to specifically support projects that help the integration of the AMU region. Tunisia's membership in the Community of Sahel-Saharan States (CEN-SAD) gives it an additional regional institutional platform that it can use to obtain a broader regional footprint and link its economy to the Sahara.

Another noteworthy regional framework is the FTA of the Great Arab Free Trade Area (GAFTA). The GAFTA's aim is to remove trade barriers among countries of the Arab League but it has been facing several challenges both at the technical level with several non-tariff barriers (NTBs) and at the political level with several countries imposing obstacles on the free movement of people and goods within the area. In addition, the difference of competitiveness levels among countries in the area has led some to undertake measures in order to protect their domestic producers in key sectors such as the agro-food, retail and electronics.

In 1995, Tunisia was the first of the "southern" Mediterranean Economic Development Agreement (MEDA) countries to sign an Association Agreement with the EU, thereby undertaking to dismantle tariffs according to a formula that resulted in 0% customs tariffs on EU industrial imports in Tunisia by 2008. Since January 2008, economic relations with the EU have entered a new phase with the arrival of the EU-Tunisia free trade agreement, the first such agreement to have been implemented with a MED country. The agreement lifts all restrictions on imports of industrial products from the EU.

In trying to push for greater economic integration in the North African region, Tunisia places special emphasis on the Agadir Process, an agreement that allows members to benefit from the diagonal accumulation of rules of origin and obtain preferential access to the EU market. Morocco, Egypt and Jordan are also members.

Tunisia has in recent years strengthened its ties with other Arab states, bilaterally and regionally, including through its membership of organisations such as the Arab League. This has facilitated beneficial new relations with the UAE, Bahrain and Qatar and has led Gulf-based companies to invest in Tunisia.

2.4. Angola case study

Economic background

Angola is located to the south of the Democratic Republic of the Congo, straddling the mouth of the Congo River at the southern end of the arc of the Gulf of Guinea oil and gas fields, in an area containing many valuable natural resources. Angola only recently emerged from a civil war that raged from 1975 to 2002. The war decimated the economy and left Angola's infrastructure in shreds, and in the post-war era, the government faces the challenge of rebuilding what was lost. In so doing, it could potentially make the most of its large oil reserves while also boosting other productive sectors. Its agricultural potential, in particular, is very important. At the time of its independence in 1975, Angola was largely self-sufficient in agriculture production and was the largest staple food exporter in sub-Saharan Africa and the third largest coffee exporter in the world. By 2000, its agriculture and mining sectors were in shreds, with landmines rendering much of the countryside unsafe, transport systems broken, and Luanda flooded with refugees from the rural areas on a scale that made it impossible to cope.

In recent years, however, Angola has become one of the world's fastest growing economies in the world, with a GDP growth rate of 20.6% in 2005, 18.6% in 2006 and nearly 27% in 2007. It received USD 15.5 billion in FDI inflows in 2008, an increase of over 50% from the previous year. This makes Angola the second top recipient of FDI in Africa, behind Nigeria which received USD 20.3 billion (AEO, 2010). Angola has used its oil wealth to drive this growth in a period of rising resource prices, especially for hydro-carbon products. Other sectors of the economy, notably financial services and construction, have also been booming. However, the global economic crisis and drop in oil revenues had a negative impact on the Angolan economy. GDP growth in 2009 dropped to 0.6% and in March 2009 the government indicated it would cut planned budgetary spending by 40%. This has had adverse implications for social projects that were in the pipeline. In all, the financial crisis made it clear that Angola needs to do more to avoid depending solely on oil.

One of the ways Angola could diversify its economy is by ensuring that its oil resources benefit other sectors. During the oil boom, there was already a knock-on effect from oil revenues on the rest of the economy, especially in infrastructure, construction and mining. Also, the Government started to support growth in agriculture, in which Angola has always had great comparative advantages, but much more needs to be done. Table 2.5 is an overview of Angola's economy. It is clear that non-oil tax revenues are only a small share of Angola's total revenue, and this share is projected to decline even further in the next few years.

Table 2.5. **Angola's economy**

	2009 supp. budget	2009 Est.	2010 Prog.	2010 Proj.
Revenues	28.5	32.5	38.6	40.5
Of which: Non-oil tax revenues	9.0	9.5	8.2	8.5
Expenditure	41.8	41.6	37.1	35.3
Of which: Current spending	27.3	28.5	24.3	22.9
Of which: Capital spending	14.5	13.1	12.8	12.5
Overall fiscal balance (accrual basis)	−13.3	−9.1	1.5	5.2
Non-oil primary balance (as share of non-oil GDP)	−51.8	−45.9	−46.8	−45.9

Source: IMF Article IV Consultation on Angola, 2009.

Angola has a vast land area that is richly endowed with natural resources and is well-positioned on the transit route between the Atlantic and its hinterland. In the same manner, Angola can utilise its location on the cusp of Central and Southern Africa to access economic opportunities from both of these regional economies. The Angolan government plays a particularly strong role in the economy, especially as its key sectors are dominated by government-controlled corporate entities. It has launched new agricultural projects and promoted various sources of finance for its private sector. Angola boasts owning one of the largest companies in Africa, SONANGOL, and the country hosts many foreign firms interested in extracting its hydro-carbon resources. However, Angola faces a key challenge in attracting investment and promoting business in non-oil sectors.

Some of the promising sectors that could be developed to a more significant level include agriculture, fisheries and livestock, and forestry. However, only 3% of Angola's arable land is utilised at present. At the same time, a variety of mining activities, including improved management of the diamond sector and the large-scale exploitation of natural gas, could be further expanded. Tourism and services are other key sectors with potential.

As part of a strategy to improve diversification, Angola needs to work on strengthening its business climate on a variety of fronts. For example, Angola is ranked 169th out of 183 countries on the 2010 Doing Business Index. It performs particularly poorly in terms of enforcing contracts, employing workers, and registering property. An ongoing challenge, in spite of a huge level of investment, is improving infrastructure by reforming the public procurement process so that only quality projects are approved. Improved infrastructure will enable Angola to utilise the expanding opportunities linked to oil, gas, and mining and facilitate the development of other sectors.

Role of government

There have been some promising developments that could boost Angola's investment prospects. The Angolan Government has been opening up to the private sector. In the financial sector, the Government has since 1991 agreed to allow an increasing number of private banking institutions to operate. Also, the Government established the National Agency for Private Investment (ANIP), whose mandate is to promote essential flows of investment that can be channelled into diversifying the economy. In May 2010, Angola received its first sovereign credit rating, B+/B1, by Standard and Poor's, Fitch Ratings and Moody's. This rating is the same as Nigeria's and Ghana's, and a few levels shy of investment grade (EIU, June 2010). Sovereign credit ratings are an important indicator of a country's attractiveness as an investment destination: the higher the grade, the lower the risk exposure faced by potential investors. Because only a few countries in Africa have been assigned sovereign credit ratings, Angola's recent development gives it an advantage over other countries in the region.

The Government has also undertaken some sector-specific measures, such as in agriculture. Here, the Government has given special priority to coffee, liquidating 33 state-controlled companies and plantations that had once been nationalised. The Government's strategy is to re-develop agriculture by removing price controls, crafting a possible rural credit scheme and creating an enabling environment for commercial farming. Also, in co-operation with development partners, the Government has established an Angolan Support Fund for Fisheries Development, and has rehabilitated a national cold-storage network. As a new approach, the Government has approved the development of the Capanda Agro-industrial Growth point in Malanje province. There have also been government efforts for initiating channels for micro-finance, such as through BDA and FND, and land reform in parallel with the privatisation of some of the largest coffee estates that were nationalised in the Seventies.

Nonetheless, the great scale of challenges in Angola calls for further government action. For example, the Government of Angola has a majority equity participation in 216 enterprises, including in sectors such as hydrocarbons, water, energy and transport. The Government is strongly centralised and this might allow it to agree on reforms quickly and to implement them effectively to drive economic diversification. However, the effectiveness of government is contingent on the improved capacities in the public service and transparency in implementing policies and regulatory initiatives.

Some of the issues the Government needs to address include: tackling problems arising from rapid urbanization in Luanda and other cities; continuing to rehabilitate and expand the effectiveness of transport infrastructure, in particular ports and railways, as well as roads;[29] increasing energy generation, and boosting access to electricity, which stands at only 20% of the population at present; constructing irrigation systems; re-writing and simplifying legislation for its growing resources sectors; clarifying land ownership; fighting corruption; increasing public sector capacities; strengthening public governance structures; and improving human resource skills. Health care and environmental sustainability are also in need of urgent attention.

In a bid to improve the use of its oil resources, the Angolan Government created the Angolan Development Bank – Banco de Desenvolvimento de Angola (BDA) – in late 2006 and soon thereafter the National Development Fund – Fundo Nasional de Desenvolvimento (FND) – administered by the BDA, to which 3% of annual oil revenues and 2% of annual diamond revenues will be channelled.[30] By the end of 2007, the BDA had approved projects with a combined value of USD 307 million. Of these, 555 were industrial, 325 for agriculture and 13% for wholesale/retail trade.

There is some concern, however, that these funds could be mismanaged, even though they are channelled via commercial banks and allocated using transparent criteria based on commercial viability.[31]

The overall transparency of the Angolan Government regarding the use of its resource wealth is patchy. While extensive data on oil matters is placed on the website of the Ministry of Finance, Angola has not yet joined the Extractive Industries Transparency Initiative (EITI). Sonangol, the state oil company, and Endiama, the state diamond company, continue to carry out quasi-fiscal operations for the Treasury and the central bank,[32] which may cause concern about the management of revenue flows. Sonangol has also been behaving like a sovereign wealth fund (SWF), using oil-based funds for investments in other countries. Examples include investments in West African iron ore mines and in Portugal,[33] as well as the purchase of oil-development rights in Iraqi oil fields in late 2009. Clearly, oil wealth is being used to strengthen the concentration of Angola's economic activity in the oil industry rather than to diversify the economy. It also illustrates the extent of the Angolan Government's presence in the economy and its potential to take action to boost economic growth and development.

Infrastructure

Infrastructure is a key component of Angola's efforts to revive its economy across all sectors following the devastation of the civil war. To develop its infrastructure, the Angolan Government has often worked in conjunction with development partners such as the Chinese Government and the World Bank, as well as key business stakeholders ranging from Chinese parastatals to Western companies.

For example, Box 2.5 describes one of the ways Angola is making innovative use of its natural endowments to rebuild after the war. However, there has been a lack of major initiatives to improve the transportation system

---

Box 2.5. **Developing infrastructure through the "Angola Model"**

Angola has been one of the four biggest recipients of Chinese financing for infrastructure projects, and indeed China and Angola's partnership in this regard has come to be known as the "Angola model" and is prevalent across Africa. Under the Angola model, the recipient country receives a loan from the China EximBank; the government then awards a contract for infrastructure projects to a Chinese firm, while also giving rights for extraction of its natural resource to a Chinese company as repayment for the loan. The terms of the loan are usually concessional in nature, with on average low interest rates (ranging from 1-6%), long repayment periods (from 5 to 25 years) and a generous grace period (from 2 to 10 years). In 2004, China extended a USD 2 billion credit line to Angola for the development of its infrastructure, which had been destroyed during the civil war. As repayment for the loan, Angola agreed to supply China with 10 000 barrels of crude oil a day. The infrastructure projects in Angola include electricity generation and transmission; rehabilitation of power lines; rehabilitation of Luanda railway; construction of ring roads; telecomm expansion; water; and some public works projects. Also, in 2006 Angola and China created a joint venture, Sonangol Sinopec International, through their petroleum companies China Petroleum and Chemical Corporation (SINOPEC) and Angola National Oil Corporation (Sonangol). The new venture aims to explore crude oil prospects in three Angolan oil fields. Angola supplies 51% of China's oil imports from Sub-Saharan Africa.

Source: PPIAF Gridlines Note 42, October 2008; "Building Bridges: China's Growing Role as Infrastructure Financier for Africa", World Bank/ PPIAF, 2008.

---

such as secondary roads in rural areas and renewable energy projects. Angola also needs to make better use of existing infrastructure resources, such as the SDI transport corridor, to facilitate trade and expand economic activities.

Natural resources

In addition to oil and gas, its main resources, Angola has huge potential in the mining and timber sectors, although the Government urgently needs to improve the relevant regulatory frameworks and build an effective public administration to support these sectors. Moreover, years of civil war have devastated Angola's bio-diversity and tarnished the country's attractiveness as a tourist destination and it will take many years to fully recover. The forestry sector is another area with a lot of potential but which was underutilised during the years of civil strife.

Human resources

Angola is in critical need of capacities and skills for industrial and agricultural development. There was a lot of labour displacement during the 25 year civil war, not to mention the disruption in education and other areas of human development. Angola's challenge is therefore to expand its economic base by boosting non-oil sectors while ensuring that its workforce is a key part of this endeavour. While the Angolan Government has prioritised capacity building, more targeted initiatives, possibly linked to supply chain management, are needed to ensure concrete results. For example, Angola hosted the Africa Cup of Nations in 2010, which offered an opportunity to boost its infrastructure and create jobs for its citizens. However, most of the benefits accrued to foreign companies instead. Angola needs to find better ways to produce more goods domestically; and improve skills among its workers so that they can undertake more service-and technology-oriented work.

Box 2.6. **Africa Cup of Nations, 2010**

"Angola has spent an estimated USD 1 bn in building four new stadiums and associated infrastructure. The work has been almost exclusively outsourced. A Chinese company using Chinese labour has been responsible for constructing four gleaming state-of-the-art venues. A UK firm has laid the pitches, the television pictures were supplied by a French company, accreditation was provided by experts from Germany and the fake shirts available on the street were made in Portugal."

Source: BBC News, 17 January 2010.

Financial resources

Angola does not have a financial services sector commensurate with its growing economy. But given SONANGOL's activities, which are quite similar to a sovereign wealth fund, there is tremendous potential for supporting Angola's financial sector and drive economic diversification.

Regional institutions

Angola is a member of three major RECs: the Southern African Development Community (SADC), the Common Market for Eastern and Southern Africa (COMESA) and the Economic Community of Central African States (ECCAS). Angola's centres of political and economic activities are mainly in the northern part of the country, but traditional ties with Southern Africa and SADC have strengthened. Angola's membership in multiple RECs could also lead to inconsistent policy initiatives, as illustrated by SADC support for the Inga hydro-power project on the Congo, which has not been co-ordinated with ECCAS despite the project's relevance to the Central African region and the Congo River Basin.

The development of the Inga III hydro-electric power project on the Congo River close to the Angolan/Cabinda borders with DRC is potentially an excellent vehicle for regional co-operation. It could also have a number of benefits for Angola by allowing it to cooperate with the DRC and Congo Brazzaville on projects that emphasise new economic sectors. The project has been spearheaded for some years by South African power utility ESKOM in a Westcor consortium which would allow power to be transmitted across DRC, Angola, Namibia and Botswana to South Africa.

However, its conceptual structuring did not account for any co-operation with Congo Brazzaville on the other side of the Congo River, nor include considerations for DRC's energy needs.

The international context

Angola has developed especially strong ties with countries other than those in the region and its major trading partner remains Portugal,[34] although its resources are fuelling economic ties with Brazil, the USA and China as well. Angola stands to benefit from these partnerships if it ensures that they are in its development interests. Angola could devise strategies to link economic projects with the transport systems being constructed by China. It could also target sustainable joint ventures with the Chinese companies involved in its territory as the DRC is attempting to do in Katanga province.

Despite the gains it has made through its relations with China, Angola appears to be failing to optimise spin-off benefits for its economy, especially for increased diversification. The dangers of this wasted opportunity were illustrated in the recent global economic crisis when a drop in oil revenues had a major negative impact on the Angolan economy, with GDP growth predictions for 2009 falling from 11.8 to 3%.[35]

With regards to EPA negotiations, Angola at first seemed to hesitate about getting involved in the process. Nevertheless, Angola has shown an increasingly active involvement in the EPA negotiations according to media and other official announcements since 2008.

2.5. Benin case study

Economic background

Benin is a relatively small country, strategically located along major transportation routes from the coast into the interior through the port of Cotonou. It is heavily dependent on agriculture, which accounts for 32% of its GDP and 70% of its workforce. One of its neighbours, Nigeria, is a much bigger economy, which offers considerable potential for leveraging various economic opportunities, in particular in relation to trade flows to and from the interior. Indeed, between 6.5 and 7.5% of Benin's GDP is derived from its trade with Nigeria. The challenge for Benin is to diversify its economy away from agriculture – and cotton especially – and to embrace economic partners other than Nigeria. Figure 2.5 outlines the composition of Benin's GDP.

Figure 2.5. **Composition of Benin's GDP**

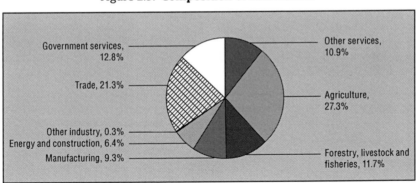

Source: African Economic Outlook, 2009.

Benin has a number of advantages in its favour. Its economy is quite stable, with an average GDP growth rate of 4% between 1990 and 2006.[36] Moreover, having a coast gives Benin the potential to become a regional transportation and services hub, especially if these sectors were co-ordinated with a greater development of its agriculture and tourism sectors. In addition, Benin is a member of the West African Monetary Union (WAEMU) and the

Economic Community of West African States (ECOWAS), which could give it an institutional platform for the diversification of its national economy. It has significant natural resources including gold, phosphates and iron, that have not been developed but which have a lot of potential all the same.

Role of government

In recent years the Government has moved away from strongly centralised control of the economy to a more liberal stance. In a 2008 report, the IMF pointed out the limited ability of the economy to absorb financial assistance, together with the need for the Government to improve its capacity to manage large scale investment programmes, especially given previous delays in capital investment programme roll-out.[37] The report also mentions that the Government needs to improve the management of structural reform and public finances, including administrative capabilities in public procurement procedures.[38]

The country has been facing a major power shortage partly because the government controlled power entity, Société Béninoise d'Électricité et d'Eau (SBEE), has been inefficient. The Government has similarly not managed to deliver on key issues such as the expansion of basic health services, payments to farmers to support agriculture activities at a time of economic crisis, and labour-intensive infrastructure projects.

Private sector

The Government took a number of steps to introduce a market-driven economy in the post-1991 period. Benin's economy performed reasonably well in recent years but has also seen greater possibilities for diversification. The relatively high real GDP growth of 5% in 2008 was largely driven by a revived agricultural sector, with cotton as the mainstay of the national economy, and high levels of trade with Nigeria. The private sector has also played an important role in boosting economic growth. The Government has made support for small farmers a key priority in terms of Government spending in 2009, along with support for labour-intensive infrastructure projects and improved health services.[39]

The shortage of entrepreneurial and managerial skills, a lack of investors in the sector, limited exploitation and development of local resources, and the unsuitable nature of the institutional and regulatory environment are the main problems holding back the country's industrial development.

Source: African Economic Outlook, 2009.

Benin was hit hard by the global economic crisis, with a severe decrease in traffic through Cotonou port and a particularly big decline in trade flows with Nigeria,[40] itself hard-hit by the slump in oil prices. In the agriculture sector, the strong dependency on cotton meant that reduced global demand in parallel with lower than expected production,[41] was a major factor that led the IMF to lower its forecast for Benin's GDP growth in 2010 to 3.0% instead of the previously projected 6%. The crisis highlighted the underlying lack of competitiveness in Benin's economy, as Figure 2.6 shows.

Figure 2.6. **Benin's competitiveness indicators**

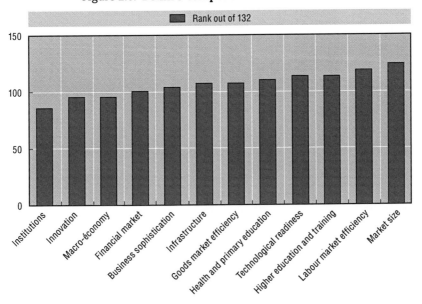

The Government needs to accelerate privatisation in many key sectors, which up to now has moved in "fits and starts".[42] With regards to the important role of small farmers, the privatisation of the country's cotton sector has also proceeded at a slower pace than expected[43] and the Government has not helped farmers to shift away from cotton as the national staple.

Infrastructure

Most of Benin's infrastructure is controlled by the state, with little private sector participation and almost no regulatory oversight. The country stands at the bottom of the list in terms of institutional reforms for its infrastructure sectors (AICD, 2010). Moreover, Benin imports about 80% of its electricity, mainly from Ghana. However, there has been some progress made in opening the sector to private investment. For instance, the Government signed a

25 year concession agreement with Bolloré Group of France for the South Wharf Container Terminal at the port of Cotonou.

The concession is expected to yield USD 200-300 million in fiscal impact; create more than 450 jobs; reduce transportation costs; and more than double container traffic in the first eight years of operation.[44] Also, in institutional terms, Benin adopted an approach of decentralised management for revenue collection, which helped increase city revenue by 82% in Cotonou. Box 2.7 also illustrates how Benin is trying to improve agricultural productivity by embracing renewable energy.

Box 2.7. **Using solar-powered irrigation to boost agricultural productivity**

Solar powered drip irrigation – also known as photovoltaic drip irrigation (PVDI) is an innovative way to deliver water to the roots of plants through a pump powered by solar energy. The technology has been used in Benin to great effect to expand irrigation in rural areas. As a result, vegetable consumption increased, food access improved, and incomes rose for the farmers who made use of PVDI. Moreover, the success of this programme has positive implications for the environment, by offering farmers an alternative to fuel-based irrigation pumps. There are also positive implications for greater – and more varied – agricultural production, especially in areas affected by water scarcity and droughts. Benin could also exploit the potential of PVDI to expand its use of internal renewable water resources (IRWR), of which Benin uses only 1.3%. To roll-out this technology, there needs to be capacity for technical services, local supply chains, and the growth of a private market and financial institutions to introduce PVDI into more areas. The benefits are worthwhile though, and bode well for diversifying Benin's agriculture sector.

Source: Based on information from "Solar-Powered Drip Iirrigation Enhances Food Security in the Sudano-Sahel Region", PNAS, Feb. 2010, Solar Electricity Light Fund, July 2010.

Natural resources

Benin has relatively limited natural resources but has fertile soils that supported a strong agricultural sector in the past, especially cotton in the north. It also has rich biodiversity, which could play a key role in boosting tourism.

Regional institutions

Benin is a member of ECOWAS, WAEMU, and through its membership of CEN-SAD, is linked to the Mediterranean via countries like Tunisia. The RECs allow for improved co-ordination in delivering regionally-based projects and improved harmonisation of standards for trans-frontier enterprises, which all stand to benefit Benin.

The International context

Benin has traditional ties with France and the EU, as well as with emerging partners in Africa such as China, Japan and the Gulf countries. China and the Islamic Development Bank are indeed already increasing their involvement as development partners for Benin.

Notes

1. As demonstrated by the country's negative growth rate following the global financial crisis.

2. South Africa is responsible for more than 17% of Africa's total output, for example.

3. In recent years, the government has provided ongoing support for the motor industry and textiles, but both seem to face structural competitiveness problems and shed many jobs during the global recession. See *The Sunday Times* (South Africa), 29th March 2009, p. 1.

4. *Source:* Africa Competitiveness Report, 2009 ; World Economic Forum; *www.weforum.org/documents/AFCR09/index.html.*

5. Examples are numerous and range from government support to transport corridors in Africa, especially within the Southern African Development Community (SADC), to the promotion of trans-frontier tourism.

6. 2010/11-2012/13 Industry Policy Action Plan; Department of Trade and Industry, South Africa; February 2010.

7. Department of Trade and Industry (2010): 2010/11-2012/13 Industry Policy Action Plan, South Africa.

8. These were the Reconstruction and Development Programme or RDP (1994); the Growth, Employment and Redistribution Strategy or GEAR (1996); the Jobs Summit (1998); the Growth and Development Summit (2003) the Accelerated and Shared Growth Initiative for South Africa or ASGISA (2005).

9. See "Trade, Industrial and Competitive Policy", in *Zumanomics*, R. Parsons (ed), Jacana Press, 2009, p. 107.

10. See R. Parsons, *Zumanomics* , *op. cit.*, pp. 187-189.

11. While this relative cost – at about 10% of GDP – is lower than the continental average, the actual bill – at USD 27 billion a year – is the highest in Africa (AICD, 2009).

12. Launched in Johannesburg on 20 October 2008, it has various South African government entities as key drivers and is using the South African tourism sector as a crucially relevant partner for international roll-out.

13. The Southern African Development Community (SADC) is composed of 14 member states located in Southern Africa and the Southern Indian Ocean, while the Southern African Customs Union (SACU) includes South Africa, Botswana, Lesotho, Swaziland and Namibia.

14. There are currently moves towards a SADC Customs Union which will have to presumably be carefully co-ordinated to avoid undermining the benefits of SACU and other overlapping regional economic communities.

15. See "From Cape to Cairo: Exploring the COMESA-EAC-SADC Tripartite FTA", IGD and FES, 2009.

16. See J. Maré, "A Time to Rationalise Southern African Ties with the European Union (EU)", *The Exporter*, South Africa, 2 February 2009.

17. It should be born in mind that some critics think that the EPAs are not in Africa's best interest and might prevent diversification, principally if several EPAs including conflicting market access regimes were signed within the same regional bloc.

18. Stated in the Kenyan Government's official response to the 2006 APRM Appraisal of Kenyan Governmental actions regarding economic governance and. Quoted in APRM, "Country Review Report and Programme of Action of the Republic of Kenya", APRM *Country Reviews Report No. 3*, September 2006, p. 191.

19. See Kenyan government response to APRM comment in: APRM, *Country Review*, *op. cit.*, p. 195.

20. IMF, Article IV, 2009.

21. Tunisia,. Share performances, Foreign Investment Promotion Agency.

22. Country Business Intelligence Reports: Tunisia, Oxford Business Group, 2008.

23. See "Tunisia Surviving the European Slump", in *The Africa Report*, December 2008/January 2009, p. 209.

24. The Airbus plant is the first outside the EU and is regarded as a particularly important mark of approval by EU manufacturers of Tunisian standards, stability and economic management.

25. Economic budget 2010, Ministry of Development and International Co-operation.

26. Country Business Intelligence Reports: Tunisia, Oxford Business Group, 2008.

27. The DESERTEC Concept describes the perspective of a sustainable supply of electricity for Europe (EU), the Middle East (ME) and North Africa (NA) up to the year 2050. See *www.desertec.org*.

28. According to the Report on the implementation of the Euro-Mediterranean Charter for Enterprise, 2008-09.

29. The inefficiencies at Angolan ports, for example, raise costs enormously and drastically undermine competitiveness, forcing shippers to think of alternative routes for exports.

30. See OECD *Report, ibid.*, p. 131.

31. *Ibid.*

32. *Ibid.*

33. See *The Africa Report*, December 2008/January 2009.

34. See OECD *Report on Angola*, p. 129, *op. cit.*

35. See "Angola's Relations with China in the Context of the Economic Crisis", *The China Monitor*, CCS Stellenbosch, March 2009.

36. Economic data on Benin from World Bank country profiles, accessed 12 July 2010, *http://web.worldbank.org/WBSITE/EXTERNAL/COUNTRIES/AFRICAEXT/BENINEXTN/0 „contentMDK:20180404~pagePK:141137~piPK:141127~theSitePK:322639,00.html.*

37. See IMF, "The Macroeconomics of Scaling-Up Aid: The Cases of Benin, Niger and Togo", IMF, September 2008, p. 5.

38. *Ibid.*, pp. 15 to 17. See also The World Bank, "Country Policy and Institutional Assessment of Benin: 2007", World Bank, 2007.

39. See: The Africa Report, December 2009-January 2010, p 204

40. See *www.worldbank.org*, Benin Country Brief 2009.

41. See *The Africa Report*, December 2009-January 2010 p. 204.

42. *Ibid.*

43. See *The Africa Report*, December 2008-January 2009, p. 180.

44. Success Stories Series – Benin: Port of Cotonou; Infrastructure Advisory Services, IFC; October 2009, *www.ifc.org/ifcext/psa.nsf/AttachmentsByTitle/PPPseries_ CotonouPort/$FILE/SuccessStories_CotonouPortWEB.pdf.*

Chapter 3

Conclusions

3.1. Building blocks for economic diversification

Diversifying Africa's economies is an important part of the continent's development strategy. This study has analysed the wide range of experiences that various countries have had with diversification, as well as the variety of factors that influence the process. Although experiences differ from country to country, there are some common findings that can be used to draw conclusions and recommendations for improved actions to support economic diversification.

Four of the case studies chosen – South Africa, Tunisia, Kenya and to a lesser extent Angola – are key players in their respective regions and beyond. The fifth, Benin, has the potential to become a regional economic hub. Analysis of these case studies reveals five critical building blocks for economic diversification in Africa. These are:

A. *The role of government leadership*

The role of Government is extremely important in Africa given the limited capacity of other stakeholders such as civil society and the private sector. Therefore, governments should aim to increase the capacity of their agencies to address impediments to diversification efforts. They also have a responsibility to be more transparent, accountable and cooperative with business, international partners and neighbouring countries. Together with stakeholders, governments can identify new products or sectors of strategic economic value, identify the appropriate resources, and facilitate the roll-out of the action plans. The Government also has to create an enabling business climate and relevant regulatory frameworks to allow enterprises to shine. The case studies have shown how these roles can be implemented in practice.

For South Africa, it is clear that the Government has played a strong role in shaping the economy and in spearheading economic diversification. In particular, it has supported new sectors such as automobile assembly for driving growth across the economy.

However, it is clear that the expertise and skills available in South Africa's strong core sectors need to be better harnessed in support of economic diversification. Too often, new initiatives have been undertaken without sufficient attention to maintaining and boosting the value of existing products and traditional sectors.

Nevertheless the Government has created a stable economic environment and a good business climate, both of which are important for supporting economic growth and creating opportunities for diversification nationally and in the region.

In order to scale up its efforts, the Government will have to address public sector capacities to support new areas of the economy.

South Africa has undertaken some successful initiatives in new fields, for example in the automotive industry. More generally, South Africa's engagement with other African economies has strengthened the region's ties with new international partners such as Brazil, India and China.

South Africa dominates the southern African regional economy, which makes it a regional hub, but also leaves some of its neighbours vulnerable to changes in South Africa's economic fortunes.

In Kenya, the Government has been less interventionist in the economy, although in recent times it has become far more active in helping to shape and support certain areas of its economy, such as in the services sector. Moreover, its public service sector remains relatively strong on the whole.

Efforts aimed at diversification have been undertaken in partnership with the private sector and other stakeholders and have mainly targeted traditional sectors of the economy. In addition, Kenya's economic initiatives have often involved a regional dimension as the country is becoming a bigger player in its neighbourhood.

In Tunisia, public policy has helped to diversify the economy, in spite of the relative scarcity of natural resources in the country. Moreover, Tunisia has made use of its geo-strategic position in the Mediterranean vis-à-vis the EU to access new economic opportunities. It has integrated itself into the trans-Mediterranean supply chain with the EU, while at the same time contributing to strengthening and diversifying the North African regional economy. By utilising its traditional economic base, Tunisia has started to develop new sectors and services. The strength of the Tunisian public service sector and the efficient implementation of economic programmes have been important in driving Tunisia's economic success.

One of the focal areas for the country's development is capacity building at all levels to support economic initiatives in the services and agribusiness sectors in order to better exploit partnerships with the EU and neighbouring countries. For example, the civil service has helped Tunisian industry in understanding and meeting EU criteria for agricultural imports. The government has also strengthened ties with the Gulf countries and has invested massively in infrastructure and urban development to improve the overall business climate.

Angola, like many African countries, has a centralised government that is heavily involved in driving the economy. It has focussed on developing the hydro-carbon sector at a time when international market conditions favoured this commodity, dramatically increasing revenues as a result. The Government has also shown increasing interest in other mineral sectors and, to a lesser extent, agriculture (the backbone of the Angolan economy prior to the civil war). Overall, there is a need to improve the quality of public service and governance mechanisms. The Government of Angola might consider using the expertise and skills it has developed in the oil sector – for example, in its successful bid for rights to develop oil deposits in Iraq in late 2009 – to bear on other strategic economic sectors.

Developing infrastructure is a key challenge for Angola in two ways: first, the Government needs to find ways to increase investment in infrastructure by building an enabling environment based on sound and transparent regulations, institutions and policies; and second, the Government has to ensure that infrastructure development does not serve only the needs of the hydrocarbon sector. Oil, gas and mining companies, many of which are China-based, are driving infrastructure development by providing the funding and expertise for constructing infrastructure assets. While these investments are welcome given Angola's infrastructure deficit, the Government should widen the scope for private sector participation in infrastructure as well.

Angola's initiatives to support economic diversification and improve the general business climate are often not broad-based or well co-ordinated. The revenues earned from oil and gas sales have made the state company SONANGOL the second largest company in Africa in terms of turnover and profits and it essentially acts as a Sovereign Wealth Fund (SWF). Yet it does not have a well-developed blueprint to guide the use of its funds for sustainable diversification of the economy, nor has it been part of broader efforts to improve Angola's business climate, with the exception of the creation of the BDA and FND. Moreover, these institutions' activities could be further improved.

Angola has used strategic partnerships with China and other countries to promote its key hydro-carbon sector, but it needs to be similarly engaged with the host of emerging economies elsewhere. On a regional basis it maintains good relations with most neighbouring countries. Nevertheless, its over-lapping membership in two RECs, Southern African Development Community (SADC) and the Economic Community of Central African States (ECCAS) remains a challenge for progress in accessing opportunities arising from its strategic location around the mouth of the Congo River/Cabinda.

While Angola has received support from China in building railway lines and port infrastructure, it has not yet optimised the spin-off effects for the diversification of its economy. Over-reliance on oil and gas exports exposes

Angola to fluctuations in global commodity prices. This was illustrated in the recent global economic crisis and the ensuing drop in oil revenues which had a major negative impact on the Angolan economy. In March 2009, the Government indicated that it would cut planned budgetary spending by 40%. GDP growth predictions for 2009 dropped from 11.8 to 3%.[1]

In the case of Benin, the Government has – despite its best efforts – been slow in taking concrete steps to support and diversify the economy. There is an urgent need to revamp key infrastructure but government efforts have been lagging and the traditional agricultural sector has suffered from the lack of investment and a sluggish international market in recent years. The Government has not responded sufficiently to the needs of many farmers, who need to diversify away from cotton into other crops. It has also not leveraged the country's potential to become a services and transportation hub in the region. In order to address these weaknesses, the local public service will need to be strengthened so that government initiatives can be better implemented.

B. The role of the private sector

In the case studies, the role of the private sector has been identified as fairly limited, with the exception of South Africa. In many cases too much red-tape and a far from ideal business climate leads to a fragile relationship between the private sector and government. Even in South Africa, which has a strong private sector and a long history of public-private dialogue, there seems to be reticence in engaging with government regarding major new initiatives.[2] Nevertheless in all of the case studies except Angola, the private sector is increasingly trying to utilise the mechanisms in place to diversify its economic activities.

In most cases, business seemed reluctant to engage government on private sector development initiatives. Similarly, interactions with regional and international institutions or stakeholders were usually limited and related to existing business ventures rather than new initiatives.

The fact that the private sector is overwhelmingly dominated by Small and Medium Enterprises (SMEs) presents a big challenge for governments because SMEs usually have limited capacity to engage with governments except through institutionalised umbrella organisations. These same structures also act as channels for capacity building measures. Nonetheless, there is insufficient engagement and dialogue, partly because government itself does not have the capacity to develop meaningful partnerships with the private sector. Only in the more advanced economies are there good examples that reveal the potential of such initiatives.[3] Privatisation on the other hand is generally endorsed by government despite differences of opinion within countries[4] but actual roll-out is erratic and slow, even in South Africa, one of the regional leaders in this regard.

C. Regional economic institutions

Throughout Africa, regional institutions have not always supported or co-operated with national governments as they undertake economic development strategies. Limitations exist in terms of capacities to analyse relevant issues and to devise relevant policy and regulatory frameworks at regional level. While there has been some effort to improve regional integration, programmes to boost regional economic diversification have been fairly weak.

The support of the EAC to Kenya's Vision 2030 nevertheless illustrates some improvement to this situation. Similarly, the initiation of a SADC regional sugar programme in 2008 was a positive step to create regional sector markets that would strengthen horizontal as well as vertical diversification. Overall, however, RECs fall short when it comes to drawing up blueprints and overseeing practical implementation required for regional diversification.

These weaknesses are further compounded by the overlapping memberships in regional institutions by many countries. Such overlaps severely inhibit action and often waste precious capacities through a duplication of efforts and a plethora of conflicting policies.[5] The 2008 initiative to turn the regions covered by COMESA, the EAC and SADC into one Free Trade Area (FTA) is a promising move towards overcoming these problems.

There is also a need for greater definition of REC responsibilities in order to allow them to gain expertise and strengthen synergies in support of diversification. The SACU, for example, has a development funding mechanism linked to revenue sharing that could be better used as a regionally structured fund in support of regional diversification.[6] The potential of SACU to become a stronger platform/anchor for expanding regional economic integration, operating at the nexus of Africa's strongest regional economic bloc, is undermined by its historic structure, overlapping membership with SADC, COMESA and other RECs, and by an understaffed secretariat.

D. The broader international context

The recent global financial crisis has shown how international events can impact on African economies including countries such as Angola and South Africa. Fortunately South Africa has been able to cushion these effects, thanks in part to its diversified and robust domestic market. Angola, however, was more severely hit and was forced to drastically cut budgetary spending.

International partnerships, such as those with the G8 and G20, could provide opportunities for driving diversification, but they have not been fully exploited. Weaknesses in the capacity of regional organisations prevent more fruitful partnerships.

UN initiatives are often focused on diversification in Africa but the ability of Africa to collaborate in order to achieve concrete results is often lacking. The SDIs/SDAs of institutions such as the AfDB offer enormous opportunities but again there are capacity problems for African stakeholders to manage their implementation.

The partnership between the EU and Africa remains important. The October 2007 launch of the EU-Africa Infrastructure Partnership is especially noteworthy as it aims to facilitate regional economic integration and diversification through African continental infrastructure projects to be finalised in 2010. Similarly, other aspects of the eight themes of a revised EU-Africa partnership, in particular partnerships on energy and science, the information society and space are important and can have regional impacts. The ongoing EPA negotiations between the EU and the ACP countries have offered further opportunities for building foundations for SSA economic diversification and strengthening integrated regional economies. The EU remains the leading development and economic partner for SSA and this support can be leveraged to foster regional economic diversification initiatives.

Nevertheless, diplomatic efforts need to be increased to tackle the remaining challenges, and in particular SSA perceptions of the risk that the EPAs could overly restrict African policy space. The EU's Everything But Arms Initiative (EBA) provides another window of opportunity for African LDCs.

The upsurge in Chinese funding for African infrastructure offers great opportunities for African countries to increase economic diversification and regional integration. Sino-African projects often are carried out on a PPP basis which leads to a greater role for the local business sector.

The Ministerial Conference of China-Africa Cooperation Forum (FOCAC), which held its fourth meeting in Cairo in , illustrates the manner in which business is being engaged in focussed dialogue. However, capacity constraints within RECs could undermine the use of Chinese projects in supporting regionally integrated economies and projects such as those linked to the transnational SDI/Ps.

Partnerships with the USA (AGOA), Japan (TICAD), India, the Mercosur, ASEAN and Gulf countries are currently not exploited to their full potential. However, the Kenyan Vision 2030, which takes the country's geo-strategic position and its international partners into account, indicates the development of more sophisticated strategies to promote diversification. This is true also for Tunisian infrastructure development and trade ties with the EU (which are often backed by Gulf funding) and South Africa's attempts to build a new niche for itself in both an African and global context.

E. Other determinants of diversification

Natural and human resources play a crucial role in economic diversification. Angola exploits its hydro-carbons but has not leveraged them sufficiently for diversification. In the case of Tunisia, the geo-strategic location and its human resource base have enabled it to pursue diversified economic growth. South Africa and Kenya are targeting diversification based on their natural resources. Lastly, Benin has struggled to achieve diversification. In all cases, financial resources are crucially important and require astute government management, especially in resource-rich countries. Investment in human resources, including its support by R&D and technology, is vital, as is the homogenisation of product standards and regulatory frameworks on a regional basis.

Infrastructure, especially transport, is a key factor that supports economic diversification in all the selected countries. The SDI/SDP initiative (supported by the AfDB) is of key relevance in this area. All the countries selected for this review have been mindful of the regional context for key infrastructural projects. For example, Tunisia has historically focused on the trans-Mediterranean region, but is now combining this with a North African focus. Other examples of regional infrastructure initiatives are the Mombasa railway link covering Kenya, Uganda, Rwanda and the DRC, and the railways from the Angolan coast to the interior. Unfortunately, Benin has fallen behind in using its regional context for economic diversification.

In all these cases, regional institutional frameworks have been used to support transport corridors, since they usually have a trans-frontier dimension. However, the RECs do not fully play their NEPAD-assigned role to drive such regional infrastructure development due to a lack of capacity. Similarly, international support for infrastructure development, for example from the EU, has not been fully exploited due to lack of government institutional capacity to interact with partners.

3.2. Recommendations

Based on the review of the selected countries and the findings noted above, there are a number of recommendations that governments can consider to improve their abilities to boost the diversification of their national economies. While these recommendations are not exhaustive they are particularly relevant in the current context of new global thinking on resilient growth promotion.[7] Apart from government initiatives, where the role of government is essential, Africa needs to prioritise and craft strategies that focus on the roll-out of effective mechanisms and programmes that are co-ordinated with all stakeholders and which can also contribute to building African capacity for sustainable results. These include: relevant capacity building measures; functional regulatory frameworks and management entities which can act as dedicated drivers of diversification initiatives at national and regional level; and policy/strategy formulation and implementation.

While all relevant stakeholders should be involved in facilitating economic diversification, the role of government remains particularly important. Primarily, governments must try to improve the business climate to support economic diversification.

A. Improved strategic management: Prioritisation, strategies/tactics, policies/regulatory frameworks and creating governance/management mechanisms

It is imperative that leading government and stakeholders identify sectors that can drive economic diversification and create appropriate strategies that are multi-dimensional in nature to achieve results. While the national economy is the point of departure, this identification process should take into account the regional dimension. Prioritisation to help focus action for optimal results is of crucial importance, given capacity shortages on many levels.

Sectoral strategies must take into consideration the sustainability and the quality of the projects. Suitable "drivers" and mechanisms to ensure continued action must be identified in conjunction with stakeholders. It is essential that all such actions should be accompanied by the crafting of relevant policies and regulatory frameworks which can be implemented and monitored by appropriate governance/management structures.

Strategies and prioritisation should also take in account pressing needs such as the current food, energy and financial crises. Meeting these needs can be achieved by, for example, embracing the global "green" economy agenda. In this respect, leveraging Africa's resources and creating an improved business climate are essential.

B. Partnerships

It is imperative that governments strengthen all existing partnerships with stakeholders internally, as well as in the region and internationally. Regular meetings and an agreement on time tables and deliverable results will improve the enabling context of projects identified to support economic diversification. Moreover, co-ordination between stakeholders at national and regional levels needs to improve. Existing partnerships must be expanded especially where gaps are identified in partnership networks. New partnerships with important economies such as Brazil, China, India and those of the Gulf could be better used by Africa and better co-ordinated with existing partnerships. In the areas of trade and investment, it is particularly important that African countries diversify their partnerships. The international community on the other hand must ensure that its actions are supportive of diversification efforts in Africa. It is essential that developmental partners strive for improved alignment and harmonisation of their policies to support African priorities, for example in trade agreements, investment policy and development assistance.

An enhanced role for Africa at national, regional and continental levels, as well as in international fora, would support the diversification agenda. However, the current capacity constraints of many African governments severely limit expanded participation. To ensure its voice is heard, Africa could draw on stakeholders and experts from the local and regional private sector, academia and civil society. Donors could contribute to a more effective dialog through multi-donor platforms for improving donor co-ordination in Africa, which in turn have positive spin offs for the private sector.

C. Support to the private sector

The private sector is the core driver of economic diversification, and thus all actions taken by government and stakeholders should aim to strengthen support to the private sector by creating a business-enabling environment. The implementation of international trade agreements, direct support in the context of PPPs, capacity building mechanisms for the private sector, and partnerships with donors and trading partners are some of the key ways governments can enhance the business-enabling environment.

Particular support should be considered for strengthening the SME sector. Its flexibility and ability to innovate and spur growth and diversification can be enhanced by improving access to finance, reinforcing links with R&D centres and business incubators, initiating contacts with peers from other countries and regions, and providing linkages with larger/multinational companies to foster technology transfer. Technology transfer can also take place at an inter-industry and intra-industrial level, so governments should support such forms of co-operation. Trade and investment flows are also crucial and relevant for strengthening the economy.

D. Governance mechanisms

To improve the business environment, it is imperative that governments prioritise enhanced regulatory frameworks and policies. In addition, national policies and regulatory frameworks should be harmonised at regional level. Another key aspect of the business environment is a functioning financial market, accessible financial services and increased domestic resource mobilisation.

E. Capacity building

Capacity building is needed at all levels. Africa needs to improve its human resources capacity, develop its social and physical infrastructure, and strengthen compliance with trade and investment rules. Capacity building measures are crucial in key categories such as general management, financial management and sector-specific technical training, marketing and promotion of government services in support of economic stakeholders, and the management of PPPs. In all cases, while government has a key role to play, other relevant stakeholders can and must play a part. Development partners can contribute by supporting capacity building initiatives to enable this enhanced stakeholder participation.

Expanding the capacity of the private sector can be achieved through business-to-business partnerships, networking, data platforms, participation in stakeholder organisations and advocacy. Peer dialogue and partnerships will be especially beneficial within a regional context and through South-South co-operation. Successful examples of the latter are the institutionalised meetings of the China-Africa Business Council and the China-Arab Conference on Energy Co-operation, or the more localised influences of Indian entrepreneurs in East Africa. In addition, relationships with the EU and Japan in the context of TICAD can be leveraged to promote South-South co-operation.

The creation of innovation centres to support economic diversification at national and regional levels offers another opportunity for governments to drive the process, especially if they are linked to centres of excellence across the continent.

Comparative market analysis will improve governments' capacities for understanding national, regional, continental and international markets to help Africa achieve and maintain comparative advantages and explore new market opportunities.

F. Regional integration

Economic diversification depends crucially on the deepening of intra-regional and inter-regional activities. Regional integration is thus a key cornerstone of any diversification strategy.

3.3. The way forward

A. Short term

The recommendations in this report should be brought to the attention of government decision makers and those in regional organisations (RECs) in Africa. They can also help to inform the work of key development and economic partners in Africa, relevant organisations in the UN system and the NEPAD Planning and Co-Ordinating Agency. Communications mechanisms include briefing sessions to relevant Ambassadors, Missions and representatives at the UN (organised by UN-OSAA) and by the NEPAD-OECD Africa Investment Initiative. The African Partnership Forum also provides a good platform to reach a variety of stakeholders.

After these "kickstart" initiatives, various African countries and RECs might consider organising discussions with leading business chambers and civil society organisations. The NEPAD Agency, in collaboration with UN-OSAA and the OECD, could co-ordinate these events on a regional basis.

The key goal of this initial short term programme would be to: i) help sensitise stakeholders about the need to seriously address economic diversification in Africa; and ii) to have some governments and RECs commit to liaising with local stakeholders to identify possible "test cases".

B. Medium term

As a next step, meetings of stakeholders and representatives of those countries/RECs who agreed to take further action should be convened. Such gatherings would discuss how to create improved business-enabling conditions for the projects. Mechanisms for "driving" the project on a sustainable basis should also be considered. A successful example of such co-operation is the Maputo Corridor Company which worked with relevant governments to create ideal conditions, attract economic players and initiate improved trans-frontier integration and economic diversification, creating the Maputo Port Company as a PPP to improve operating conditions. The corridor could serve as a blueprint for other infrastructure projects such as in the Bas-Congo and the Mozambican Nacala Corridor. Selection of projects should be co-ordinated with key infrastructure SDPs of the AfDB, the RECs and national governments.

C. Long term

In the long term, projects should aim to be sustainable and act as blueprints that trigger similar initiatives in other African countries or sub-regions. The AfDB and OECD Secretariats, and the NEPAD Agency, together with UN-OSAA, could identify lessons learnt and promote an expansion of economic diversification activities to the sub regions. In all these deliberations, the private sector and civil society must be represented.

Notes

1. See "Angola's Relations with China in the Context of the Economic Crisis", *The China Monitor*, CCS Stellenbosch, March 2009.

2. The UNOSAA study "The Private Sector's Institutionalised Response...", *op. cit.*, gives further detail in this regard.

3. Such examples would include the NEDLAC of South Africa, the NESC in Kenya and various structures in Tunisia.

4. South Africa and Benin are good examples of how trade union movements have often questioned ongoing privatisation initiatives by government. The reverse is also true: in 2009, in South Africa, the trade union movement and Communist Party of South Africa opposed calls for nationalisation of mining and other sectors.

5. This is a politically controversial issue, yet the AU/NEPAD agree that there are problems in overlapping REC memberships that must be resolved.

6. Noted by South African Trade and Industry Minister Robert Davies in an address on 12th October 2009 at the South African Institute for International Affairs (SAIIA) in Johannesburg.

7. The recommendations listed are largely those decided upon at the UNOSAA Expert Group Meeting on Economic Diversification in Africa: A Review of Selected Countries, held at UNECA, Addis Ababa from 17th to 18th November 2009.

Abbreviated Bibliography

Publications

Alden, C. and G. le Pere (2004), "South Africa's Post-Apartheid Foreign Policy: From Reconciliation to Ambiguity", *Review of African Political Economy*, 31 (100): 283-297.

Africa Peer Review Mechanism (2006), *APRM Country Review Report No. 3: Republic of Kenya*, Midrand, September.

Africa Peer Review Mechanism (2007), *APRM Country Review Report No. 5: Republic of South Africa*, Midrand, September.

Ayangafac, C. (2008), *Political Economy of Regionalisation in Central Africa*, Institute for Security Studies, Pretoria.

BBC News (2010), "Angola Uses Football to Showcase Economy", 17 January, *http://news.bbc.co.uk/2/hi/business/8463972.stm*, accessed 8 July 2010.

Corkin, L. (2009), "Angola's Relations with China in the Context of the Economic Crisis", *The China Monitor*, CCS, Stellenbosch, March.

Department of Trade and Industry, South Africa (2010), *2010/11-2012/13 Industry Policy Action Plan*, February.

Dube, O., R. Haussman and D. Rodrik (2007), *South Africa: Identifying the Binding Constraint on Shared Growth*.

Government of Kenya, (2008), *Kenya Vision 2030*.

Institute for Global Dialogue and Friedrich Ebert Stiftung (2008), "From Cape to Cairo: Exploring the COMESA-EAC-SADC Tripartite FTA", IGD and FES.

Lighthelm, A. (2007), "Structure and Growth of Intra-SADC Trade", Research Report No. 358, Bureau of Market Research, UNISA.

Nairobi Ministry of Metropolitan Development (2008), *Nairobi Metro 2030*, Ministry of Metropolitan Development.

Nest, M., F. Grignon and E.F. Kisangani (2006), "The Democratic Republic of Congo: Economic Dimensions of War and Peace", *International Peace Academy: Occasional Papers*, Lynne Reinner, London.

OECD and AfDB (2010), *African Economic Outlook*, Paris, Tunis.

OECD (2008), "South Africa: Economic Assessment", *OECD Economic Surveys*, July.

Parsons, R. (ed) (2009), "Zumanomics", *Jacana Press*, Johannesburg, 2009.

Southern African Development Community (2006), *Regional Indicative Strategic Development Plan*, SADC, Gaborone.

The South African Institute of International Affairs (2004), *Business in Africa Research Project Reports*, SAIIA, Johannesburg.

United Nations (2002), Final Report of the Panel of Experts on the *Illegal Exploitation of Natural Resources and other Forms of Wealth of the Democratic Republic of Congo*, New York, October.

United Nations, COMTRADE *database, www.un.org.*

United Nations Economic Commission for Africa (2007), *The 2007 Big Table: Managing Africa's Natural Resources for Growth and Poverty Reduction.*

United Nations Economic Commission for Africa and African Union (2007), "Accelerating Africa's Development through Diversification", *Economic Report on Africa 2007.*

United Nations Office for the Special Adviser on Africa (2006), "The Role of the Private Sector for the Implementation of the New Partnership for Africa's Development".

United Nations Office for the Special Adviser on Africa (2007), "The Private Sector's Institutionalised Response to NEPAD: A Review of Current Experience and Practices".

World Bank (2000), "Trade Blocs", *Oxford University Press*, New York.

World Bank, *World Development Indicators*, Washington DC, various years.

Periodicals

African Connexion, South Africa.

African Investor Magazine, London, UK.

Centre for Chinese Studies Briefing, CCS, Stellenbosch.

ECDPM acp-eu-trade.org e-newsletter, ECDPM, Maastricht.

Financial Mail, South Africa.

Gabon, London.

NEPAD Dialogue (electronic), Midrand, South Africa.

Newsweek.

The Africa Report.

The China Monitor, CCS, Stellenbosch, South Africa.

The Courier, European Commission, Brussels, Belgium.

The Economist.

Tradewinds, Institute for Global Dialogue (IGD) South Africa.

Time.

Newspapers

Business Day, Johannesburg, South Africa.

The Exporter, Johannesburg, South Africa.

The International Herald Tribune, Paris (European edition), France.

The Star, Johannesburg, South Africa.

The Sunday Times, Johannesburg.

The Times, London, UK.

Universo, SONANGOL.

Country-level consultations through country missions to:

Angola, Kenya, Tunisia, and South Africa.

ORGANISATION FOR ECONOMIC CO-OPERATION AND DEVELOPMENT

The OECD is a unique forum where governments work together to address the economic, social and environmental challenges of globalisation. The OECD is also at the forefront of efforts to understand and to help governments respond to new developments and concerns, such as corporate governance, the information economy and the challenges of an ageing population. The Organisation provides a setting where governments can compare policy experiences, seek answers to common problems, identify good practice and work to co-ordinate domestic and international policies.

The OECD member countries are: Australia, Austria, Belgium, Canada, Chile, the Czech Republic, Denmark, Estonia, Finland, France, Germany, Greece, Hungary, Iceland, Ireland, Israel, Italy, Japan, Korea, Luxembourg, Mexico, the Netherlands, New Zealand, Norway, Poland, Portugal, the Slovak Republic, Slovenia, Spain, Sweden, Switzerland, Turkey, the United Kingdom and the United States. The European Commission takes part in the work of the OECD.

OECD Publishing disseminates widely the results of the Organisation's statistics gathering and research on economic, social and environmental issues, as well as the conventions, guidelines and standards agreed by its members.

OECD PUBLISHING, 2, rue André-Pascal, 75775 PARIS CEDEX 16
(20 2011 01 1 P) ISBN 978-92-64-03805-9 – No. 58011 2011-01